SLEIGH RIDE TO RUSSIA

The front cover picture is of No 34 panel 'Deputation to the Czar 1854', taken from the new Quaker Tapestry, designed by Debby Mason and the Tapestry group and worked by Griselda Mary Mason of Plymouth.

ISBN 0 900657 99 5

Phototypeset and printed by William Sessions Limited
The Ebor Press, York, England

SLEIGH RIDE TO RUSSIA

An account of the Quaker Mission to St. Petersburg
by Robert Charleton, Henry Pease and Joseph Sturge in 1854
to present an address to Czar Nicholas
from Meeting for Sufferings
to try to avert the outbreak of the Crimean War.

by

Griselda Fox Mason

WILLIAM SESSIONS LIMITED
YORK, ENGLAND
1985

Contents

Illustrations

Drawings on pages 31, 50, 90, 106, 118 by Debby Mason

Acknowledgments

First I would like to thank the family, 'Dear Octopus', without whose help and encouragement this project would never have been started; and without their patience and persistence in teaching me how to use a word processor the book would never have been completed.

Next I would like to thank my many friends, with a large and a small F, who have lent me letters, books and pictures, and given generously of their time to help in my researches.

As this book records an incident in the history of the Society of Friends I have in the spirit of George Fox, the founder of the Society, omitted all honourable prefixes and academic distinctions and just listed my chief benefactors: Lloyd and Griselda Fox, Michael and Yvonne Fox, Tom and Alex Fox, Joseph Gainford, Henry Glaisyer, Joan Lawson, Dorothy Mounsey, Edward Milligan, Eric Denton, Murdoch Ritchie, Roger Angerson, and to all others too many to mention: Thank you.

Amberley House   Griselda Fox Mason
Plymstock
Plymouth
1985

Foreword

by Lord Gainford of Headlam

Joseph Edward Pease 3rd Baron Gainford of Headlam in the County of Durham succeeded his father in 1971. In 1973 he was a delegate to the United Nations working on the Human Rights Committee.

The title was given to his grandfather, Joseph Albert Pease, in 1917 for political services, who was an M.P. for 24 years holding several government posts including President of the Board of Education. He continued his public service as a member of the House of Lords for 26 years, a family tradition carried on by his grandson the present Lord Gainford, whose special interest is in transport.

It is my great privilege to write a foreword to this book. In addition to it being my privilege it is another cause for my pride in being a member of the Pease family. The Peases became one of the leading families of the nineteenth century. They became a byword in business industry and politics.

It was through their influence, particularly that of my great-great-great-grandfather Edward Pease of Darlington that railways became a vital part of transport in Britain. The success of the Stockton and Darlington Railway, opened in 1825, thanks to the genius of George Stephenson and the foresight of Edward Pease, led to the construction of the Liverpool and Manchester Railway and its opening in 1830.

Transport and industry boomed because of the work of the Peases. Darlington and Middlesbrough, two vital towns in the North East of England, owe their existence to them.

Joseph Pease, son of Edward, became the first Quaker M.P. Others followed, including Henry, who plays such an important part in this book. But the particular point of this story is how men, who not only hated the thought of war, through their belief and consciences did what few men can claim to have done. They went to the highest authority of the country that was on the point of becoming the enemy of their own country. If they had succeeded where diplomats and politicians failed, the history of Europe in the years that followed and in the next century might have been very different.

Henry Pease not only influenced his own country. He took that influence abroad to where few British people had travelled.

It is thanks to the author that a new light is shone on the Crimean War. It is another vital example of historical research. Because letters and documents once sealed up in family vaults are becoming available, history becomes a living thing, not just something that is part of a dreary text book.

To read this book is like having a telescope to view, close up, a special part of the last century.

In commending this book to all its readers I wish them many hours of combined study and pleasure in the certainty that it will teach them something valuable.

Marlow, February 1985.

Gainford

Introduction

Other people's letters are far more interesting than one's own morning post, especially letters written one hundred and thirty years ago from St. Petersburg the capital of Czarist Russia. These letters were written by my great great uncle Robert Charleton to his wife Catherine née Fox, by my great grandfather Henry Pease to his son and other members of his family, and by my cousin Joseph Sturge. They give a vivid account of their winter journey across Europe, and reveal something of the hopes and fears of the delegation, who left London on 20th January 1854 with an Address from the Society of Friends to present to the Czar.

The most often quoted account of this journey, written by his sister-in-law Anna Fox, is the *Memoirs of Robert Charleton*, published by Samuel Harris and Co., in 1873. This book includes most of his letters in an edited form, from which, as was common in Victorian biographies, the beginning and end of the letters and all family references had been omitted. In this book, the original letters, where they exist, have been printed in full with the postscripts, and the writing across the page added as another postscript.

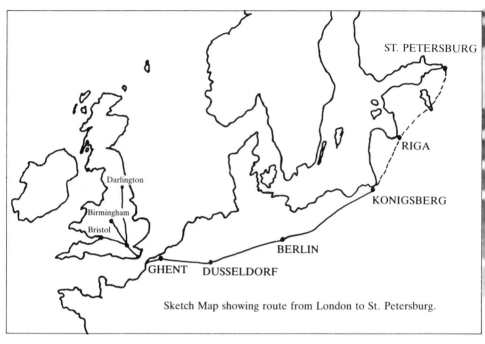

Sketch Map showing route from London to St. Petersburg.

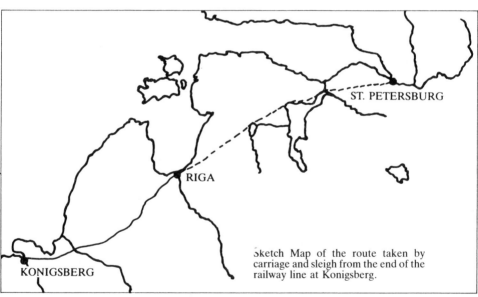

Sketch Map of the route taken by carriage and sleigh from the end of the railway line at Konigsberg.

x

CHAPTER I

Why Visit the Czar?

ON THURSDAY, 2ND FEBRUARY, 1854 at seven o'clock on a cold, dark, winter evening a carriage attached to a sledge arrived in St. Petersburg, the capital of Imperial Russia. Inside were three middle aged, middle class Quaker gentlemen, no doubt tired and hungry, but thankful to have arrived safely, for they had travelled nearly two thousand miles. It was an arduous journey, by ship across the channel, by train to the end of the line, then by coach, and finally when the snow became too deep the wheels were removed and sledge runners fitted instead. The three Quakers were my cousin Joseph Sturge of Birmingham, my great great uncle Robert Charleton of Bristol, and my great grandfather Henry Pease of Darlington. The object of their journey was to try to prevent the outbreak of war between England and Russia.

Russia was already at war with Turkey. At that time Turkey was a weak state, often referred to as the 'Sick man of Europe'. Ten years before in 1844 Czar Nicholas had proposed that Britain and Russia should divide the Turkish Empire. Britain was to take Egypt and Crete, and Russia was to occupy Constantinople and to be the protector of the Balkan provinces cf Moldavia, Wallachia, Bulgaria and Serbia, their independence to be guaranteed by the Great Powers. In 1853 similar attractive proposals were made to the British Ambassador in Russia, Sir Hamilton Seymour. Britain turned down these suggestions, not for any high moral scruples, but because she feared the increase in Russian power. If Russia controlled the Bosphorus, her warships would have free access to the Mediterranean and could threaten the British trade routes.

Another cause for conflict between Russia and the Western Powers arose over the question of the Holy Places in Jerusalem. Traditionally, since the time of the Crusades, these had been looked after by French Roman Catholic Monks, but during the French Revolution the Greek Orthodox Church had taken over the guardianship. In 1853 the new Emperor Napoleon III of France, anxious to curry favour with the French Catholic Church, persuaded the Turkish Sultan to recognise the claims of the French Monks. Czar Nicholas retaliated by demanding the restoration of all privileges for the Greek Monks and that he should be recognised as the protector of all Christians in Moslem Turkey.

These demands threatened Turkish sovereignty. The British Ambassador in Constantinople, Lord Stratford de Redcliffe, was determined to oppose the Czar. There is no evidence that he had positive instructions from the British Government, but he encouraged the Sultan to stand firm and implied that the British would support Turkey if war broke out. The British Prime Minister, Lord Aberdeen, did not want war, but he ordered the fleet to Besika Bay outside the Dardanelles. The situation deteriorated when Russian troops occupied Moldavia and Wallachia, the Turkish provinces on the border with Russia.

To try to prevent further conflict, a conference was held in Vienna by the Western Powers of Austria, Prussia, France and Great Britain. The Vienna Note was drawn up and sent to the Sultan and the Czar. The Czar was prepared to accept the proposals, but the Sultan encouraged by the 'hawkish' Lord Stratford refused to accept the demands and declared war on Russia in October 1853. Russia retaliated by attacking the Turkish naval base at Sinope. The Russian warships fired French manufactured high velocity incendiary shells, a 19th-century 'exocet' missile, which destroyed the Turkish fleet. The western press called the Russian victory 'the Massacre of Sinope', although as the two countries were already at war it could hardly be compared to the treachery of Pearl Harbour. It resulted in 'Russophobia' in London and Paris, and an increased chance of the escalation of the conflict. England and France issued a joint demand on 22nd December that the Russian Fleet should take no action against Turkey and the allies sent their own fleets into the Black Sea in order to enforce the demand. The tense situation had become critical. Most people in Britain thought that war was inevitable; indeed many clamoured for the destruction of the Czar.

The war feeling in Britain was created by the Whig leaders, especially by Lord Palmerston, and by the *Daily News* and the radical press; it was supported by some Tories who opposed their peace loving leader Lord Aberdeen. The British healthy dislike of despotism, especially strong among the Victorian middle class, was directed against Russia rather than Turkey, because Russia had helped Austria to suppress the Hungarians in 1849, and Turkey had sheltered Kossuth the Hungarian leader and other Hungarian refugees. A war with Russia was said to be necessary in order to preserve the integrity of the Ottoman Empire and the balance of power in Europe. Cobden and Bright were the only men of mark who had looked behind the curtain of Turkish misrule at the 'chamber of horrors euphemistically termed the Ottoman Empire'. They considered that the war if undertaken would be not merely unnecessary but on the wrong side, because our troops would be used to keep the Christian population subject to the Moslem Turks. This was a minority view and one which was becoming increasingly unpopular. The changing attitude of the press can be shown by the Sheffield papers, which in July 1853 had talked of peace and praised the Prime Minister, but were demanding war in December; 'Mere talking to the Czar will do nothing, now the time does appear to be at hand when we must act so as to dissipate the evil designs and efforts of Russia'.

There were some Quakers who believed that good might still come from talking to the Czar. They did not regard the Czar as the embodiment of tyrannical oppression, because Quakers had had several contacts with the Czars. This started when Czar Peter the Great, supposedly incognito, visited England on a fact finding mission. He worked in the shipyard at Deptford to gain first hand knowledge of how to build a navy, while in London he met several Quakers, and attended Gracechurch Street Meeting. Later in 1814 Czar Alexander I paid a surprise visit to Westminster Meeting. He was so interested and impressed by what he saw that he decided to employ a Quaker, Daniel Wheeler, to drain and cultivate the crown lands around St. Petersburg. He talked to William Allen and Stephen Grellet, and from these interviews it seemed clear that the enigmatic Czar and the quiet Quakers had much in common. Czar Alexander had died in 1825 and it was not known whether his brother Czar Nicholas I would be so sympathetic towards Quakers, but any action which might prevent the horrors of war was worth trying.

The idea of appealing to the Czar seems to have originated with Joseph Sturge of Birmingham. His biographer Henry Richards relates that:

> In December 1853 while Mr. Sturge was in earnest conversation with his friend Mr. Joseph Cooper the idea was started whether some good might not be effected by a deputation from the Society of Friends waiting upon the Emperor of Russia.

Joseph Sturge was sixty, an age when it might be expected that a Victorian gentleman would spend most of the winter in the comfort of his own home and not driving across the coldest part of Europe. He must have been a determined character with a strong constitution probably due to his healthy life in the country as a boy. Joseph Sturge was born in 1793 the second son of Joseph and Mary Sturge who were Quaker farmers. He was one of a family of twelve, eleven of whom survived. His testimony against war was tested at an early age when he was drawn for the Militia to fight in the Napoleonic wars. He refused to fight. Instead of going to prison he returned home one evening and saw his valuable flock of sheep being driven off his farm. Perhaps it was this experience which turned him against farming; he became a corn factor. He started his business at Bewdley in Worcestershire where he made a home for his brothers and sisters when his parents died.

3

In 1822 Joseph Sturge moved to Birmingham, which was becoming increasingly important as a business centre. He lived first at Monument Place where his firm had an office from which to control its expanding and increasingly successful business. Later he moved out to Edgbaston. In 1834 he married Eliza Cropper, the daughter of a Liverpool merchant, but tragically his wife and baby died within a year. It was twelve years later in 1846 that he married Hannah, the fourth daughter of Barnard and Ann Dickenson of Coalbrookdale. Joseph and Hannah Sturge had one son and four daughters.

Joseph Sturge worked hard as a corn merchant, but early in his career he made up his mind that he was not going to spend all his time and energy making money. As his business prospered he spent more time in political work as a candidate for Parliament and as an Alderman for the growing city of Birmingham, where a Memorial Statue was erected by his fellow townspeople as a mark of gratitude for his devoted work, Like many Quakers in the 19th century Joseph Sturge took an active interest in the abolition of slavery. The slave trade had been abolished in 1807, but there was a long struggle before the slaves in the West Indian Islands were freed in 1834. Although free in theory they were not free in practice, because a tragic mistake was made in the Act of Parliament which set up the apprenticeship system. This ordered the slaves to work for their old masters for seven years before they were quite free. The former slaves were paid wages, but were forced to work long hours in bad conditions and cruelly treated if they refused. Reports were reaching England of this cruelty, reports which were not always believed. All staunch abolitionists were determined to end the apprenticeship system as soon as possible, in spite of the opposition of the colonial legislatures. In order to find out at first hand what the situation was in the West Indies, Joseph Sturge and Thomas Harvey decided to go on a fact finding mission. It was a dangerous journey not only because of the long voyage by sea, but also because of the hostility of the plantation owners to any interfering abolitionists from England. The slave owners had received compensation for freeing the slaves and they did not want it to be proved that they had failed to carry out the terms of the Act, which might have resulted in their losing the slaves and the money. Joseph Sturge visited Antigua, Montserrat, Barbados and Jamaica talking to people and trying to find out at first hand the conditions of the former slaves.

When he returned to England he brought with him a young boy whom he had rescued from the apprenticeship system. They toured the country and Joseph Sturge made many speeches drawing attention to the conditions in the West Indies. He also published a book *The West Indies in 1837* the first edition of which was sold out in a few months. His work helped to convince the government that they should end the apprenticeship system. In politics Joseph Sturge was an advanced Liberal, an advocate of manhood suffrage, of the removal of all religious and civil disabilities and of complete freedom of commerce. He stood as a Member for Parliament on these principles, first for Birmingham where he was defeated by a considerable majority, and later for Nottingham and Leeds where he was narrowly defeated.

Joseph Sturge was interested in many philanthropic causes such as Education, Juvenile Reformatories, and the abolition of the Opium traffic. In the obituary notice in the *Illustrated London News* it says:

> His ear was never deaf nor his hand closed against any tale of distress. His kindly nature was widely and warmly appreciated even by those who new little of him, and whose quick, active step, cheerful voice, and genial smile will long be missed by those amongst whom his busy, useful, self-denying life was passed.

Throughout his life Joseph Sturge was an active member of the Peace Movement. The London Peace Society was formed in 1810 during the Napoleonic wars; two years later he started a branch in Worcester. He attended and spoke at many Peace conferences including the one held in Frankfurt in 1850. From there he went with Elihu Burritt, the well known American pacifist and Frederick Wheeler to visit the leaders on both sides, in the attempt to prevent bloodshed.

Perhaps it was this experience of diplomacy which made Joseph Sturge feel that he should lead a deputation from the Society of Friends to appeal to the Czar. In 1850 his efforts were praised by his friend Richard Cobden who wrote:

> You have done good service by breaking through the flimsy veil with which the diplomatists of the world try to conceal their shallow craft, by your startling expedition to Rendsburg and Copenhagen . . . You have done good work never mind the sneerers.

Cobden's attitude in 1853 had changed and he had become most unsympathetic:

> I don't think you ought to encourage the idea of sending a mission to the Czar. Your business lies with the people of Birmingham.

Less than a week later Cobden writes even more forcefully:

> I rather think you overrate the effect of deputing to crowned heads. Friends have been charged with being too fond of the 'great', and the *Memoirs of Allen,* and other biographies, give some colourable sanction to the suspicion that you have 'tuft-hunters' among your body. If a party of Friends were now to set off on a visit to Nicholas, it might I think expose them to a charge of seeking their own

glorification. Nothing short of a miracle could enable such a deputation to accomplish the end in view; and miracles are not wrought in our times.

This seems a reasoned argument for not visiting the Czar; if Joseph Sturge had listened to his sensible friend there would be no story to tell, but he was not deterred by discouraging letters from doing what he thought was right, so he brought his concern to Meeting for Sufferings.

As Mike Yarrow explains in his book *Quaker Experiences in International Conciliation* (Yale University Press) the word 'concern' has a special significance in Quaker use; it means the religiously inspired impulse to put God's love into action in some concrete situation. Concerns sometimes arose out of a Meeting as a whole. More often an individual would submit a concern and in the quiet of worship ask if he were following the right 'leading'. If the group found unity with the concern they might help it forward. If not, they might still stand behind the individual as he carried out his concern or 'moved as the way opened'. If definitely opposed, they might appoint a committee to wait upon the individual and try to point out the error of his or her ways, a process called 'Eldering'.

Early in the organising process committees took on an important role, frequently performing functions that in other religious groups fell to the pastor. Committees functioned at Monthly Meetings, Quarterly Meetings, and Yearly Meetings. They were selected by nomination and approved in the business meeting. While Quakers have as many jokes about committees as others do, they also have a high regard for their potential.

> The concern of an individual should be laid before the worshipping group, so that corporate guidance may be given by an expression of unity or disunity.

The grandfather of all committees was Meeting for Sufferings, a group of representatives from many Monthly Meetings. Originally organised for defence against persecution, Meeting for Sufferings became, in effect, an executive committee for London Yearly Meeting, acting between annual sessions.

Meeting for Sufferings met in London on Friday, 6th January, 1854. They supported the idea of sending a deputation to Russia, and appointed a 17 man committee to draft an Address to Nicholas. They also had to find two other suitable Friends to accompany Joseph Sturge.

One of the members of the drafting committee was Samuel Fox, whose niece Catherine was married to Robert Charleton a well known Bristol Quaker. Samuel Fox wrote to his nephew, and this is the reply.

Robert and Catherine Charleton

7

My Dear Uncle,

I am in receipt of thy letter of yesterday. I send a few lines by this evening's post, as I am going to Sidcot School tomorrow morning, with the prospect of not returning until fourth day morning.

It is impossible not to admire the Christian devotedness of our dear Friend Joseph Sturge, in thus offering to go to St. Petersburg, on this truly benevolent yet arduous mission: and it would be a very great relief and comfort to me to hear of his being provided with two suitable companions. But in the event of two such companions not being obtained, and the concern of the meeting being thereby in danger of falling to the ground; I believe I should not feel easy to decline the proposal to accompany him, should such a proposal be made to me by the Committee of the Meeting for Sufferings. At the same time I do not feel enough to warrant my offering myself to engage in this service, I should be truly thankful to be excused from it, if this can be done without prejudice to the concern of the Meeting, a concern with which I cordially sympathise.

Perhaps thou will write me again by third day evening's post, so that I may receive it on my return from Sidcot on 4th day morning. My dear Catherine unites with me in love to thyself and Aunt, to whom she is indebted for a very kind and interesting letter received yesterday.

I am thy affectionate Nephew

Robert Charleton

Notwithstanding which I have written, I cannot but fear that the time for availingly interposing our good offices in this matter is past, but of this of course you will be better able to judge, after seeing our Government, and the Russian Ambassador.

This letter reveals a great deal about Robert Charleton, the conflict between his own feelings and his sense of duty; clearly he is a realist, not optimistic about the chances of success, but prepared to put aside his own comfort to support his friend Joseph Sturge. Robert Charleton was the eldest and only surviving son of James and Elizabeth Charleton. His two brothers were drowned in a shipwreck off the coast of America in 1836. They may have been on their way to stay with their Uncle and Aunt, James and Lydia Fuller of Skaneatles. There are several letters to Robert Charleton from his Uncle and Aunt and cousins but none which refer to the tragedy.

Information about the two younger Charleton boys can be found in a page of a family pedigree written by their father James Charleton on p. 110 in the Appendix.

As a boy Robert spent some time in the South of France, where his parents went to spend the winter for health reasons. He attended a day school and as he says:

> I was the only English boy; and being obliged to use the little French I knew, I soon got to speak it pretty fluently, almost as easily as speaking English.

This must have been very useful as French was the language of diplomacy. On their return from France they lived for a time at Penzance where his mother died in 1826. His father remarried in 1835 Elizabeth daughter of Thomas and Sarah Fox, the Quaker woollen manufacturers of Wellington, Somerset. James Charleton died in 1847 but Robert continued to reside with his widowed stepmother until his own marriage at the end of 1849; it was no doubt through his stepmother that he met her niece Catherine Brewster Fox the eldest daughter of Thomas and Catherine Alexander Fox, my great great grandparents. The inter-marriage between Quaker families was very common, as members could not marry anyone outside the Society and still remain members.

Robert Charleton was trained as a Land Surveyor and Agent in the office of H. F. Cotterell, a Friend at Bath. He then moved to the Kingswood area of Bristol as a pin manufacturer. It was said that he took over the business in order to prevent a considerable number of people being thrown out of employment. The brick buildings from which he carried on this work and his house at Two Mile Hill are still there. He was a liberal employer who tried to help the needy population by which he was surrounded. Robert Charleton founded and supported from his own resources two large schools in different parts of Bristol. He also assisted in the management of Sidcot, the Quaker school in Somerset.

Mere business pursuits did not occupy all his time and energy, but if his worldly business did not bring him wealth it brought him what was far better, the means to do good to his fellow men, temporally, morally and spiritually. He could afford to retire from business at an early age in 1852 and devote all his time and a large proportion of his income to philanthropic work. His income was from wise investments, probably in railway shares, and certainly exceeded his personal and family expenditure, even after he moved to 3 Ashley Down in 1853. Anna Fox writes:

> That locality had been from early years especially attractive to him, from its retired and rural character, and the beautiful shrubs and trees in the grounds were a source of continued and healthful interest his taste and skill being often exercised in judicious pruning planting etc.

9

We are not told how many gardeners or garden boys he employed to help him with his hobby. He was also fond of country walks and interested in astronomy. He had two or three holidays on the continent, to the Lake District, and Scotland, to enjoy the mountain scenery. He visited Ireland with Samuel Capper, a well known Quaker preacher to help to arrange religious meetings, but was horrified at the poverty he saw there.

At home in the Bristol area Robert Charleton was well known for his support of the Temperance movement. He was the first person to sign the total abstinence pledge, a frequent speaker and chairman at Temperance meetings, and he often introduced the subject in addresses on other occasions when suitable opportunities occurred. He lectured on the evils of drink, and tried to help in a more practical manner by assisting some poor families to start a new life in America. There is a fascinating letter from one of these families. Mr. Woodruff, writing from Skaneatles in February 1848, described his family's early struggles to get work and make a living in their new country (see Appendix p. 112).

The Woodruff family were not the only people who Robert Charleton helped in this way. There is an equally interesting letter from Ham and Eliza Brown (see Appendix p. 115).

The humble gratitude of these people is surprising considering the hardships they endured in America. But they saw it as a land of opportunity, and it is an indication of the terrible conditions which they had left behind in England that they were prepared to suffer the dangers of the transatlantic crossing, and to work hard to make a new life for themselves and their families.

Helping the poor and working for the Temperance Movement were not Robert Charleton's only interests. He was also concerned with the Quaker testimony against war.

The Peace Society was supported by him at a local level in Bristol, and nationally and internationally. He spoke at their annual meeting in London in 1850, and attended the International Peace Congress, held in Frankfurt later the same year, at which Joseph Sturge played a prominent part. In February 1853 Robert Charleton presented an address from the Conference of the Friends of Peace at Manchester to the Prime Minister, the Earl of Aberdeen. 'They were received', writes Henry Richards the Victorian biographer, 'not only with courtesy, but, we may truly add, with real cordiality, and his lordship assured them that he had never met a deputation in whose objects he more entirely agreed.' The Earl of Aberdeen might have been sympathetic to Peace delegations, but he does not seem to have been capable of controlling the warmongers even in his own party. The connection with the Peace Society made Robert Charleton known to a wider circle of Friends, so that he would be recognised as a suitable person to accompany Joseph Sturge on the mission to Russia.

When his Uncle Samuel Fox mentioned Robert's reluctant offer to the drafting committee of Meeting for Sufferings it was accepted. The drafting committee did not waste any time, they asked Meeting for Sufferings to consider the draft of the Address on Wednesday, 11th January. At that meeting the draft of the Address was altered slightly and approved; the drafting committee were then instructed to see that the Address was duly signed and to arrange for its presentation. On Tuesday, 17th January, a Special Meeting for Sufferings chose Joseph Sturge and Robert Charleton of Bristol as members of the deputation. The selection of a third member was left to the drafting committee, the spot for his name being left blank on the commission. It is not known who asked Henry Pease of Darlington, my great grandfather, to be the third member, or when he decided to go, but it was known by Thursday, 19th January. On that day Edward Pease wrote in his diary in true Quaker phraseology that his son Henry:

yielding to the desire of the Meeting for Sufferings goes along with Robert Charleton and Joseph Sturge with a memorial to the Emperor of Russia, I suppose imploring him to put a stop to the effusion of blood and human misery now affectingly carried on with the Turks.

Henry, the youngest of Edward and Rachel Pease's eight children was born on 4th May, 1807; both his parents were Quakers, whose 'outward engagements were always kept subservient, and regulated by their religious duties'. When Henry left school he was apprenticed to a tanner, his parents thinking that the manual work in the tan-yard would be better for his health than a more sedentary occupation; no doubt they worried that he was outgrowing his strength as he was six foot three. After he had finished his apprenticeship he left the tan-yard, thankful to escape from the unpleasant smell, and joined the family woollen business making frequent journeys in the north of England and Scotland for wool buying and for orders.

The main interest of Edward Pease and his family was the development of the railways. In spite of strong opposition, Edward Pease and his friends were granted an Act in 1821 to build the Stockton and Darlington Railway. The first object of the company was to transport coal using horse power. In 1823 the Act was ammended to allow the use of an entirely new power, that of locomotive engines. George Stephenson was appointed engineer and became a frequent visitor to the Pease family home at Northgate. A locomotive foundry was started at Newcastle where the first engine was built. Horses and engines were used at the outset. It was not until the work was well advanced that anyone thought

11

Henry Pease

of carrying passengers. On 26th September, 1825, Edward Pease and his sons made a trial trip on the new railway; but on the great day of the opening ceremony they had to stay at home behind closed blinds because Henry's brother Isaac had died in the night. Mary Pease, Henry's second wife wrote in her story of his life:

It was a striking instance of the mixed nature of all earthly things, often experienced afterwards by Henry Pease in his long life, but never more acutely felt on this day of victory and rejoicing, sore sorrow and bereavement.

At sixty-three Edward Pease retired from all direct management in railway affairs so that Henry's time was increasingly occupied with the extension of the railway system in his neighbourhood: the planning and inspecting of new lines over, in some cases, difficult country, suited his energetic and practical temperament. His responsibility for the family business was further increased after 1832 when his elder brother Joseph was elected to Parliament and became the first Quaker to take his seat as an M.P. It is almost incomprehensible to us today to understand how great a commotion the bare idea of a Quaker standing for Parliament caused in the Society of Friends. There was a tremendous opposition especially from his nearest relations. Joseph Pease, to calm his mother-in-law Jane Gurney's feelings, wrote:

I will not canvass, I will not ask one man for his vote, I will go to no expense, I will both in and out of Parliament unflinchingly support my practice and my profession as a member of the Society of Friends; if elected under these circumstances I will endeavour to serve them faithfully.

This he did, being re-elected as a Liberal M.P. until he retired in 1841.

There was no such outcry when Henry Pease decided to stand for Parliament in 1857, although Edward Pease wrote on Monday, 6th April:

Considerable excitement in the town, the Sheriff declaring the election of Pease and Vane. My mind does not derive comfort from dear Henry's election, but as an increase of virtuous right-minded men in the House of Commons is greatly to be desired, so I desire that merciful overruling goodness may permit some enduring good to spring out of what my dear son does consider to be his right and important station.

Henry Pease was a Member of Parliament for eight years until 1865, and his son Henry Fell Pease was later Member of Parliament for Cleveland.

In 1835 Henry Pease married Anna Fell, only daughter of Richard and Mary Fell of Uxbridge; their only son Henry Fell Pease was born on 28th

13

April, 1838, but Anna, who seems to have been delicate, did not regain her health and strength, and died in July 1839. Edward Pease wrote:

Received the account of the decease of my Beloved daughter in law Anna, who died at St. Leonards on the morning of sixth day last. Very sweet is the remembrance of this amiable-minded daughter her end was peaceful, her resignation and patience in a long, wasting illness proved a fine disposition and well regulated mind. My dear Son, after a very endearing union of four years, becomes a Widower at the age of thirty-two with one only son.

The baby son was brought up by his maternal grandmother until her death in 1846. Then he returned to Darlington to live with his father, who had just moved into Pierremont a large house on the outskirts of the town. This was described by Edward Pease as a 'showy mansion' for which his son had paid '£5,000 a fair price'. Henry enjoyed improving his new property especially making a garden on a piece of ground opposite his house which he called Pierremont South Park and which was open to visitors.

It was from Pierremont that Henry Pease and his son travelled to London, to spend a hectic day buying the fur clothing needed for a mid-winter journey to Russia. They stayed at William Hughes' house in London with Joseph Sturge, Robert Charleton and their wives, ready to make an early start on Friday morning. While there Henry wrote to 'My Dear Brother', almost certainly his eldest brother John and his wife Sophia, whose loving sympathy and Christian counsel he mentions gratefully in his journal.

It appears that this was the first opportunity that he had to read the Address, and his comments are interesting. He points out that neither the British government nor the Russian Ambassador had been informed of the object of the mission, as it was to be stressed that it was a religious mission. The Meeting for Sufferings committee must have decided on this policy of telling the British government after the delegation had left, perhaps they feared that they might be prevented from leaving.

Letter from Henry Pease to his brother John

HUGHES 19/1/54

My dear Brother,

I feel that my strength has been rather taxed: I cannot make much of a letter.

We had this evening, J. Hodgkin, R. Forster, and J. Pease, J. Cooper, also J. Sturge's and R. Charleton's wives are here – the

Hughes – sat with us, and I hope a time of some right feeling, when ministry and supplication were heard amongst us, and kind remarks of sympathy from T. Norton and others.

There has been a great business trying on furs etc., we go at 8 a.m. to-morrow. There is every reason to believe that a letter posted on the 7th day afternoon at Darlington would find us at the Hotel Saxe, Berlin.

I have read the Address, it is uncompromising but respectful, possibly fully long. It has been thought better to look upon this simply as a religious mission, so neither our Ministers nor the Russian Ambassador have been informed of the object of the mission. With very dear love to dear relations,

Your affectionate brother,

Henry

John Pease

CHAPTER II

To the End of the Line

ON FRIDAY, 20TH JANUARY at 8 a.m. Joseph Sturge, Robert Charleton and Henry Pease left London by train for Dover, on the first stage of their long journey. The speed with which the final preparations were completed is amazing; it must have been quicker and easier to go to the Foreign Office and obtain a hand-written passport signed by the Foreign Secretary than it would be now to obtain all the documents needed to repeat the journey in the 1980's. There was no question of being able to book a through ticket to St. Petersburg; they did not know which would be the best route to take from Berlin; whether they would travel via Warsaw or to Konigsberg, the end of the railway line in East Prussia. They had letters of introduction to people who were business associates of Friends who might be able to help them on their journey, although Richard Cobden maintained his disapproval and declined to give his friend Joseph Sturge a letter of reference to anyone.

Joseph Sturge was not very optimistic about their chances of reaching St. Petersburg, it seemed very likely that war might break out before they arrived at their destination. On the eve of the day of their departure Joseph wrote to his brother:

> Thou canst have hardly less hope than I have of good from our mission, and it seems more than probable that we shall have to return before getting to Petersburg. I may be wrong but I have scarcely an anxiety of personal safety, either from the climate or from the Czar, beyond the ordinary uncertainty of human life.

Although he did not fear for his personal safety, he did mention his will in his letter, and with remarkable thoughtfulness at such a time, he left detailed directions on two matters concerning the welfare of his fellow citizens; the proposed establishment of a Temperance Home for sailors at Gloucester, and the supply to his employees of flour at a rate below the market price, which was then very high. It was typical of Friends that they should try to leave their affairs in order before going off into unknown dangers. There must have been in all their minds the fear that war might break out, perhaps before they could reach St. Petersburg, or while they were there, so that they might not be able to return home; they might have been imprisoned in Russia until the end of the war. They had no diplomatic status and therefore no diplomatic immunity.

Robert Charleton in his first letter written from Dusseldorf says that at the special evening Meeting they had at William Hughes' house where they were staying, John Hodgkin advised them not to be concerned about the rumours of war. John Hodgkin was a well known Quaker, who often spoke in Meeting with great intellectual force; he also had a voice of singular strength and clearness, so that an elderly Friend said to him: 'we thank thee for speaking so loud; thou art the only Minister in Meeting whom we always hear'. The support and encouragement of Friends, especially the members of Meeting for Sufferings, must have strengthened the resolve of the delegation to carry out their mission.

This first letter is from Catherine Charleton's book, so that it is mainly a factual account of their journey. They were fortunate to have mild weather. Edward Pease had noted in his diary for the beginning of January that the weather was very cold, but obviously it had thawed by the 20th, so that the first stage of their journey was easy and uneventful.

The phrase 'First day' refers to Sunday; 'Second day' to Monday and so on. This method of writing the days of the week was used by most Quakers, to avoid using names derived from heathen gods. As strict Quakers they did not travel on Sundays, but kept it as a day of rest, when they wrote letters and had their own little Meeting, in this case with a local Friend, Auguste Mundencke. Joseph Sturge felt so strongly that people should not work on Sunday that he resigned as one of the Directors of the London to Birmingham railway because his fellow Directors and shareholders decided to run trains on Sundays.

Letter from Robert Charleton to his wife, Catherine

DUSSELDORF 1 MO 21 1854 ON THE RHINE

You will have heard by a telegraphic message of our safe arrival at Calais, and after an agreeable journey through Belgium, by way of Ghent where we lodged last night, we arrived this evening between 8 & 9 o'clock. The weather has been delightfully fine both yesterday and today, and remarkably mild. The snow has mostly disappeared and the ice on the Rhine, which was lately of great thickness, is now entirely gone and the noble river flows along with much the same volume as I have been accustomed to see it in the summer. It became dark soon after we left Aix-la-Chapelle this evening; and the sky being very clear the Planet Venus, shone with such brilliance that I thought I could perceive a shadow from it, not withstanding the motion of the carriage. Hitherto the journey has been performed in a very pleasant and unfatiguing manner; we may, perhaps, be laying in a stock of vigour for encountering the fatigue which will necessarily attend the Russian part of our route.

First day morning.
What I have written relates only to the incidents of our journey; but I have not been without serious recollections and thoughtfulness as to its object. We must not, as John Hodgkin remarked, be much concerned about rumours of war, but steadily go on with the object before us, relying on such help as may be mercifully granted us for carrying it out. It is a comfort to refer to the truly interesting religious opportunity with which we were favoured at W. Hughes' on the evening before I left.

Afternoon. We had an agreeable sitting this morning at Auguste Mundencke's. Before sitting down, A.M., in conformity with his usual practice, read one or two chapters in the New Testament very agreeably, and it was, I hope, not an unprofitable little meeting.

Before 8 o'clock on Monday morning the three travellers caught the train to Berlin. Trains in 1854 did not have corridors or refreshment cars, so that they had scheduled stops for meals, just as there had been with stage coach travel. Robert Charleton in his letter from Berlin is impressed by the speed and efficiency of the German railways. He says that it is not very inferior to the Great Western Express, which was Brunel's broad gauge train, acknowledged to be of superior speed and generally easier motion at high velocities than the narrow gauge trains. The German railways used the narrow gauge similar to that used in most of Britain.

Henry Pease, who had expert knowledge of railway systems also praises the German trains. In his letter from Berlin written to his brother John he says:

Our run of about 380 miles from Dusseldorf to this place was in all respects performed in a style well calculated to lower an Englishman's pride as to railway management, 14 hours in to the moment.

Anyone reading these letters written in the middle of the 19th century will be surprised not only by the speed and efficiency of the trains but also of the postal service. A letter written in London by Hannah Sturge on Saturday reached her husband in Berlin by Tuesday, 24th January; so they had welcome news of their families both by letter and by telegraph. They were informed that Joseph Cooper, a prominent member of Meeting for Sufferings and a personal friend of Joseph Sturge had had a satisfactory interview with the British Cabinet Ministers. Although on a religious mission Friends needed to keep in touch with the British Government in case war broke out. The travellers were able to telegraph to Friends in London that their route would be via Konigsberg, the capital of East Prussia and the end of the railway line.

Robert Charleton started writing his letter to his wife early in the morning and finished it later in the day, a method he often used in order to give the most up-to-date information before catching the post. It seems as if he was enjoying his travels, but had to remind himself from time to time of the serious object of the journey.

This letter gives an idea of the way in which letters of introduction worked. A letter given to them in London by Cornelius Hanbury, a Director of the Quaker firm of manufacturing chemists, Allen and Hanburys, introduced them to August Beyrhaus. He took them to see Pastor Gossner who had lived in St. Petersburg and was able to give them letters of recommendation to people he knew there. A chance meeting at the hotel with a young English merchant enabled them to have a letter of introduction to a friend of his at Riga. These local residents were able to help and advise the travellers. It also made their journey more interesting as they were shown places such as a private hospital and schools which would not have been seen by ordinary tourists.

In Catherine Charleton's version of this letter she leaves out the unfavourable comparison between English and German heating systems; perhaps she disliked the implied criticism of the 'low temperature produced by our English mode of warming'. I do not know what method of heating was used in the Charleton's home in Bristol, but I remember how cold The Court, the Fox family home in Wellington was when I stayed there in the 1930's. Clearly Robert enjoyed the warmth, while Henry Pease disliked the stuffy atmosphere.

Catherine also omits any reference to letters and telegraphic messages received; so she probably left this out of the letter from Konigsberg. The original letter from there has not survived so that I can only reproduce Catherine's edited version. Telegraphic messages were exchanged as this is mentioned in a Meeting for Sufferings' minute. It was important that they should know the latest diplomatic situation before they crossed the Russian frontier. The end of the railway line was also the end of the telegraphic line as the two systems were developed together. How surprised and horrified the 1854 travellers would have been if they could have seen the destruction of 'the handsome city of Berlin' and the Berlin Wall.

Letter from Robert Charleton to his wife, Catherine

HOTEL DE SAXE BERLIN 1 MO 24 1854

My Dearest Love

I hope thou duly received my letter from Dusseldorf despatched on first day. We spent the evening at Auguste Mundencke's very

20

pleasantly, and left for this place yesterday morning agreeably to our intention. We passed through Minden, Hanover, Brunswick and Pottsdam, arriving at Berlin soon after 9 o'clock. Had there been time and our minds differently occupied, it would have been very pleasant to spend an hour or two in several of the above towns, so interesting in themselves, and so rich in historical associations. As it was we saw next to nothing of any of them, passing rapidly along, and the later part of the journey being performed in the dark. The whole distance from Dusseldorf to Berlin is about 375 English miles, and was performed in about 13 hours, including stoppages for meals. This is a rate of speed about equal to that maintained by the fast trains on most of our best appointed English railways, and not very inferior to the Great Western Express; while the strict punctuality, and capitally good arrangements in every department, exceed anything I have before witnessed. On arriving at Berlin, we found the space in front of the Railway Station covered with slippery ice, and the double windows, and white porcelain stoves in the bedrooms of our Hotel, indicate that we are passing into a colder climate. Porcelain stoves are the most agreeable means of warming a room that can well be imagined. They diffuse equable warmth over every part of the room, without dust, or a particle of that disagreeable and unwholesome smell which proceeds from iron stoves. The houses are kept much warmer than in England; and were I to spend a winter in Germany, I fear I should be spoiled for the comparatively low temperature produced by our English mode of warming. It does not, however, appear to make the people at all tender; they seem as hard and robust as could be desired, certainly as much so as our own country men. I have written the above early in the morning before breakfast and meant to conclude towards the evening. It is very pleasant to hear from our friends in England and of their kind solicitude for our preservation and welfare. It is also comforting to hear of thee, in a short note written by Hannah Sturge to her husband; for though it was written only a day after our departure, it feels gratifying and refreshing to receive a message from my dearest, even after that short interval. A telegraphic despatch is just come in for Joseph Sturge from Joseph Cooper, as follows; 'The three families quite well. A satisfactory interview with the Government'. We shall telegraph back in the course of the day, after we have decided to go either by Konigsberg or Warsaw, in order that you may have the opportunity of telegraphing to Konigsberg should that be needful or desirable. Although from the uncertainty of our route, I could not arrange for thee to direct letters for me this side of Petersburg, yet the foregoing despatch will in some degree supply the lack of such intercourse; the information that it conveys is none the less welcome from being so laconically expressed.

Afternoon. We have decided to go by way of Konigsberg, and have sent a telegraphic despatch to Joseph Cooper accordingly. We shall leave this evening at half-past-ten, and if all be well, arrive at Konigsberg at half-past-six tomorrow evening. We have been with a letter of introduction from Cornelius Hanbury to Auguste Beyrhaus, who received us with much cordiality, and took us to the Pastor Gossner, a venerable old man of 85, who formerly lived at Petersburg, and gave us a letter of recommendation which may be useful to us there. We also went over a private hospital under Pastor Gossner's care, supported much in the same way as George Muller's Orphan House. The truly Christian spirit which prevails in the establishment made our visit quite an interesting one. Berlin is a very handsome city, with good wide streets abounding with public buildings, some of them quite magnificent. There was a hard frost last night, and it still freezes in the shade; but owing I suppose to the dryness of the atmosphere, it does not seem nearly as cold to the feelings, as it would with the corresponding temperature in England. We have had a delightfully fine day for getting about in the city and doing the various business requiring attention before proceeding further. We met at the Hotel an Englishman, a member of a house engaged with Russian trade at Petersburg and Riga, and who has very kindly furnished us with a letter of introduction to a friend of his at Riga, which we shall probably find useful. I may remark, on the whole, that we have experienced great civility and kindness from all those persons to whom we were furnished with letters of introduction, or with whom we have made aquaintance on the journey. It is not unlikely that I may write again either from Konigsberg or Riga, I am meanwhile, with love to Father, Anna, Aunt El, and our other relatives,

thy truly affectionate husband,

Robert Charleton

Letter from Henry Pease to his brother, John

BERLIN, 24/1/54.

My Dear Brother John,

Ample as was the proof of thy deep interest in my taking part in this formidable mission, I yet feel as if there was something egotistical in

22

supposing that it would be worthwhile for thee to wade through another batch of my notes, having posted to our dear Father 1st day. But I cannot forget on an outward bound journey every day that elapses adds 'so much' to the time the next letter requires to reach the same destination as the former. Accept then my message as proof of affection, and not of egotism.

Our run of about 380 miles from Dusseldorf to this place was in almost all respects performed in a style well calculated to lower an Englishman's pride as to railway management, 14 hours in to the moment. I do not yet see much increased aspect of winter, some of the railway cuts have large quantities of snow, and stagnant waters are covered with unyielding ice. Here it is very frosty with ice in the streets, but the paths are so neatly sanded, that there is no inconvenience. We keep our eyes and ears open to learn the state of things and after so much travelling since 6th day it seemed almost startling in taking tea last evening to find printed in a Berlin paper of the day, the price of funds in London say at 2 o'clock, from this it would seem that the fear of war preponderates, and it was not the less pleasant this morning to have our own Telegraphic message stating that Friends in London had had a very satisfactory interview with the Ministers and we understand by this, that the Ministers did not wish to prevent our attempt.

Now I will give thee a few of the reports we hear. That an article has appeared in the *Times* and one in the *Monitor* arguing, that in the event of Russia declaring war, Prussia cannot be neutral and it is added that the said articles are semi-official.

That Prussia is not for war at all, that if the King declared war the soldiers must go, but that the money would not be easily found for what the people do not approve, and that they have now more voice in government than formerly, that the feeling is much against Russia, and with some hope that if war takes place a rebellion would break out in Russia. That the Emperor has caused an inscription to be put over a gate at St. Petersburg 'The way to Constantinople'; but there are points probably more correct than these reports viz:– that the Emperor has of late given way to a religious enthusiasm and imagines he is to destroy the Mohammedans in Europe and regrets that he has so long delayed. His eldest son is said to be mild and pacific and for Russia liberal. The second son approves of this war desiring Constantinople as his capital. There seems no doubt that young men are kidnapped at night in Russia and sent off to the army. So vast is the horror and misery that seems to open to the view, one feels ready to say, 'How long?' in writing to St. Petersburg do not refer much to Russia, it is understood that letters are opened. We shall be asked at

23

the frontier, if we get there, if we have any sealed letters we shall be able to answer 'No', how we shall do when examined about our errand we do not quite see, if we say to present an Address, then perhaps it may be taken from us and sent on which would not at all answer. However, it must be concealed on the person and be got in if at all possible. We have prospered here in obtaining information relative to our journey. A young Englishman came to this Inn last night who has been seven years in Russia and from him we have sundry particulars, beside those from a very competent and civil official at the post office, and there is now no doubt as to Konigsberg being the best route. Our journey may be as follows, leave here, Berlin 3rd day, 10.30 p.m. by rail to Konigsberg, arrive 6 p.m. 4th day at —————— on 5th day, 6th and 7th, 36 hours journey to Riga there on 1st day, 2nd, 3rd, 4th days and nights continuously to St. Petersberg. There is no reason to suppose we can do better than this probably our own carriage on sledge from Riga may be best and cheapest.

This would make just two weeks work with reasonable rest, (barely) to reach the point, however our labour would be naught if good could be done, duties are ours. I have today thought of Ayton Committee and its interests, I have thought in so long an absence from home, of dear relatives and that only child so dear to me. But I have no sense of being out of my lot, this is something, and we three go to-gether very harmoniously – in health on the main – and have fine weather outside, hitherto warm rooms as German stoves only can warm a room, but these with double windows, constant cigar smoking, makes a close house. We paid an interesting call to Professor Gossner at 8, he gave us an introduction to a chamberlain of the Emperor; we also visited his hospital for seventy-three sick persons all on the voluntary principle, very nicely managed. I felt my sister Sophia's kind note.

Dear love to loving Nieces.

Thy Brother as ever,

Henry

Letter from Robert Charleton to his wife, Catherine

KONIGSBERG FIRST MONTH 26TH 5TH DAY MORNING EARLY.

We left Berlin on 3rd day night about 11 o'clock and arrived here between 7 and 8 last evening, a distance of 420 miles. The journey was performed all by rail, with the exception of about 12 miles between

24

Dirschau and Marienberg, i.e. between the eastern and western arms of the Vistula, which was performed in a diligence with horses, the railway bridge over the river and the intervening line not yet being finished. We drove over the Vistula on the ice, the track for carriages being indicated by rows of branches stuck into the ice, which had much the appearance of young trees growing; this together with the rough uneven surface of the snow, on both sides of the track, gave it so much the appearance of land, that it seemed difficult to imagine ourselves on a deep river. The ice on the Vistula has for many weeks been thick enough to bear the heaviest carriages without danger; and, in case of a change in weather, the river is so closely watched and means to obviate the danger so carefully applied, that accidents appear never to happen. We are all three remarkably well, this bracing atmosphere suiting us thoroughly. We are now about 1200 miles from London, and have about 600 more before reaching St. Petersburg. Owing to the diligences being generally full, and travelling by day and night without stopping, we mean to obtain a carriage and post it, which is the most agreeable, and for four persons travelling together, the most economical way of proceeding. We have been favoured to get on hitherto with both safety and comfort, and we may well trust that all needful care and protection will be mercifully extended to us for the future. In order not to cross the Russian frontier in the dark, which would be the case were we to start tomorrow morning, and thus be detained all night about the examination of luggage etc. we have decided to set off this evening and travel through the night. Konigsberg is a rather interesting old town, with a population of about 80,000 inhabitants. The corn trade carried on here, though much less considerable than at Dantzic, is still very large, and there are warehouses of sufficient extent to store about 600,000 quarters of wheat. The vessels are, of course, locked in the ice, and the streets of the town are covered with snow, which, by treading and freezing, is become extremely hard and compact. Many passengers and goods are conveyed over it on sledges, but more, I think on wheels which can easily be exchanged for a sledge whenever the state of the roads make it desirable. It is impossible for us to do otherwise than feel the responsibility of the duty we have undertaken, yet I think that we are all in cheerful spirits, and able to take a hopeful view of the future, relying in some degree, I trust, on the continued watchful care of our Father in Heaven.

Robert Charleton

Konigsberg was the capital of East Prussia, which was joined to West Prussia when the heiress married the ruler of West Prussia in 1618. The two regions of Prussia were divided by part of Poland, until Poland was partioned by her greedy neighbours at the end of the 18th century. Poland, although great in size, had a very weak government. In 1772 Catherine the Great of Russia entered into a dishonourable conspiracy with Frederick the Great of Prussia and Maria Theresa of Austria to seize Polish territory on the pretext that the Polish government was unable to keep order. By the partitions of 1793 and 1795 Poland disappeared from the political map of Europe until the Treaty of Versailles after the first Great War. Thus in 1854 Prussia and Russia had a common frontier near Tilsit. Konigsberg is now called Kalingrad and is in the U.S.S.R.

The problem for railway travellers in the mid-19th century was very similar to motorway travel earlier this century; travel was quick and easy until some unfinished part of the line. For travellers to Konigsberg the bridges had not been built over the river Vistula; as long as the frost held this was not too serious, as a horse bus took the passengers across the ice, but if there had been a sudden thaw, as was feared on their return journey, they might have had to make a long detour to cross at Warsaw. Unfinished parts of the line were just as common in England as on the continent. For many years travellers from Bristol to Exeter had to get out at Wellington, Somerset and go by horse and carriage over the White Ball hill, until the tunnel was completed, while Brunel's great railway bridge over the Tamar was not built until 1859.

Henry Pease's letter written to his niece Elizabeth Pease Gibson gives more details of the journey, including the price of the first class train fare from Berlin to Konigsberg. This worked out at 2d per mile, which was considerably cheaper than the usual stage coach price of 5d per mile for an inside seat and 3d per mile for a seat on the top. This meant that by 1854 travel by train was not only quicker and more comfortable, it was also cheaper. One disadvantage of coach travel was that if the coach was full the inside passengers were uncomfortably crowded, also all classes travelled together; with railways there were first, second and third class carriages. Knowing the disadvantages of stage coach travel it is not surprising that the delegation decided to hire their own carriage.

Letter from Henry Pease to his niece, Elizabeth Pease Gibson

KONIGSBERG 5TH DAY 26/1/54

My dear E. P. Gibson
In the brief notice I had before leaving for this journey, I saluted my dear relatives at Walden with a short notice, and it is a pleasure to have pen in hand thinking of thee surrounded I hope by blessings

26

innumerable, for thine has been what we term a favoured lot; but possibly I might not have asked thee to accept this from thy Uncle H., had I not written twice to Darlington and feared that if I wrote again so soon they would think I magnified my own importance, and truly no such temptation is upon me, so thou seest dearest E. if when you write to D. you say you have heard of me from hence, this will be enough; and I have one other little commission in order that my dear H. may feel that when his father forsakes him some care for him, just write to him and I shall be obliged, and he will be pleased, and may be dear F.E.G. would do so too. Surely parents can only understand the place that dear boy has with me. I can scarcely bear to think that almost every day I am hundreds of miles further away, and even should we progress favourably we cannot expect to be here again much within a month! We might go to America in less time.

Our first days work was from London to Ghent, on 7th day to Dusseldorf what handsome places these are as I believe thou knowest, 1st day at Dusseldorf, second day at Berlin 380 miles, third day until 11-30 pm. at B. then through the night to this place 420 miles, at 7-30 pm. We have reason to speak well of the railways here, good speed, punctuality, a steady motion, and luxurious fittings, warmed, and charge £3 yesterday 1st. class, not 2d per mile. There is a stage of about 10 miles including crossing the Vistula on the ice by diligence, the bridge over the Vistula for the railway is building, will require about three years yet; the tracks over the ice are indicated by small trees on each side, so except for ships fastened in, you might suppose it was simply a flooded meadow on each side.

Thou canst suppose how grand a thing it is for the inhabitants of this place of 80,000 to be able to communicate with, or travel to, their Capital within 24 hours, compared with at least a week's uneasy journey formerly. Well so far so good we may say, and last evening I proposed that a post should be erected at the station at this place, 'Here European civilization ends'. So little seems to be known of Russia that our days delay in Berlin was with a view to obtain information. Amongst our calls was one on Pastor Gossner, who gave us a letter to a Chamberlain of the Emperor N. We then visited Gossner's hospital for 75 sick persons, a titled lady and a lot of Sisters do all gratuitously, food and clothing excepted. The former was a most pleasant efficient looking person and the sisters looked much like a group of young women Friends, I said gratuitously but as some of these have married some of Gossner's missionaries perhaps I was not strictly correct. As regards weather we have as yet nothing more severe than we have had in England, but our large fur cloaks, and fur boots to the knees, were none too much coming from Berlin. There is

27

here just so much snow that the lively tinkle of sleigh bells is, as I write, perpetual, but wheeled carriages are also numerous. The streets are in an uncomfortable state, old heaps of ice and snow, in the narrower streets some pools of water. There are here several buildings of rather imposing size, but I have seen no interesting architecture, there is a very finely executed bronze equestrian statue of the late King of Prussia, duly guarded by a soldier. The export of corn is the chief trade of this place, there are long lines of high posts and pannel gable-ended granaries, coloured a dull red, these store 800,000 qrs of corn. We have had very fine weather, the sun shines cheerfully on my paper as I write. We have had a long round to procure a carriage, and the owner rather grieved us, adding £5 for the hire after he saw he had English to deal with. We tried 3 other places in vain and have been considerably perplexed to find out the best road from this to St. Petersburg, but have at length concluded to go by Riga and Dorpat, and as the Russian boundry is about 12 hours from here, and it would be inconvenient to be there at midnight, we conclude to leave at 10 this evening, so as to be there in the morning. The distance to Riga is 210 miles, we wish to be there on 1st day, and by leaving to-night and travelling on 6th day night we hope to be in on 7th day, then we have 400 miles to St. Petersburg, and hope that by travelling night and day (3rd day night at Dorpat excepted) to be at St. P. on 5th day. We carry considerable varieties of stores, and a samavar, or urn kettle, with us. The search of our things will be very strict, not even a parcel in a newspaper will be allowed and as for an old favourite testament I do not know whether to take it or leave it, but to be perhaps at St. Petersburg without it would be disappointing.

I shall probably write home from Riga, as the time from thence to St. P., and the return of a letter would make it seem long at home; I have had none since I left, it is just possible there may be one before we leave to-night, if not I fear it can not be until we reach St. P. As to our errand dear what can I say, the case is an awful one, I do not think so far as human reason goes any right to expect to see fruit. It may be that the most High permits the Emperor to be thus warned, and I do not doubt it is right that a Christian community as Friends should maintain this testimony against War: it is of no importance, comparatively, how the bloodshed is prevented if only it be so.

Very dear love to each from your uncle, and to thy Uncle and Aunts if they will accept it.

Thy truest,

Henry Pease

CHAPTER III

News from England

FORTUNATELY ROBERT CHARLETON's letter from Riga has survived, as it is one of the most interesting, not only for the details of the journey but also as an insight into his thoughts. Clearly he is longing to receive a letter from his wife and to know what is happening in England. He writes across the front page of his letter as a postscript the instructions as to when and where she should write so that he will hear from her on the return journey. This shows remarkable confidence in the efficiency of the post.

The reference to the way they are ridiculed by the London papers is left out of Catherine Charleton's extracts. The press attacks on the mission must have been harder for the families at home, than for the travellers who try to make light of the matter. Certainly there was no hope of keeping such a mission secret. *The Times* on Monday, 23rd January wrote under the title *Turkey and Russia:* 'A deputation from the Peace Society has just left England for St. Petersburg to endeavour to induce the Czar to come to terms with Turkey. The deputation consists of Mr. Henry Pease of Darlington, Mr. Joseph Sturge of Birmingham, and a gentleman from Bristol whose name we have not heard'. It was probably from this short paragraph that other papers copied the mistake that the delegation was from the Peace Society. The reference to Elihu Burritt's *Olive leaves*, was to the well known American Quaker, who was nicknamed 'the learned Blacksmith'. He had formed the League of Universal Brotherhood in 1846 and organized peace congresses; he also went with Joseph Sturge to mediate in the Schleswig-Holstein Denmark crisis.

Henry Richard, the secretary of the Peace Society, was quick to issue a disclaimer in a letter to *The Times;* he denies any connection with the delegation and any knowledge of the nature of their mission. This disclaimer seems strange in view of Joseph Sturge's active participation in the Peace Society.

The Times printed a correction: 'The deputation which has left England for St. Petersburg we find is not from the Peace Society but from the Society of Friends. The deputation consists of Mr. Henry Pease of Darlington the brother to the late M.P. for South Durham, Mr. Joseph Sturge of Birmingham, and Mr. Charleton of Bristol'. *The Times* referred to the deputation as a piece of enthusiastic folly, other papers and periodicals were more vicious and scathing in their comments.

The Darlington and Stockton Times writes:

We certainly have no faith in the success of their mission; the love of peace has not yet penetrated the cold regions of the north sufficiently to thaw the Autocrat into such a melting state as to induce him to pay much attention to the theories of the British Peace Society, however good they may be.

Sturge is written about in the same grudging way by *The Birmingham Mercury*:

His mission, though a mistake, is a most amiable one. His benevolence, though pure waste, is still benevolence.

The Bristol Mirror and *General Advertiser* for Saturday, 25th February writes:

Those well meaning but deluded individuals Messrs. Pease, Charleton and Sturge, have had an interview with the Emperor of Russia. The scene was just what might have been anticipated. The deputation were polite to the Czar, who, in return, was quite affectionate in his reception of them, shook hands heartily, and insisted on introducing them to the Empress. Both parties seem to have been mutually pleased, but at present we are quite in the dark as to any results good bad or indifferent from the perpetration of this piece of enthusiasm. However the deputation have shaken hands with a live Emperor and will doubtless be extremely popular at Sunday tea tables when they return to relate their experiences.

Their local papers were scathing or damned with faint praise, but the attack in *John Bull* was far more vicious especially the construction which it inferred should be placed on their motives:

With all their simplicity we suspect that the Friends are much too shrewd a race to have imagined for a moment that any practical effect would result from this mission. If so, knowing that they were going on a bootless errand, wherefore did Mr. Sturge, Mr. Pease and their nameless Bristol brother go at all? Was it to parade themselves before the world as more righteous than the rest of mankind? Or simply to gratify their sectarian vanity, by showing what consequential people they are with whom even such a man as Czar Nicholas will shake hands?

Punch published several short paragraphs under such headings as:'Save us from our Friends', 'St. Petersburg Theatre', 'A Pilgrimage to Russia' and 'Feathers in the Broadbrim'. A longer article was headed *The Doves of St. Petersburg* and ended with the sentence: 'And such is and has been the policy of the Czar, to treat for peace, while his dove-like thoughts sit upon bullets'.

The Doves of St. Petersburg

This attitude was to be expected from the hawkish majority in England, what is more surprising is that the *Herald of Peace,* the official publication of the Peace Society did not print an article praising the efforts of the deputation until March, when the Quakers had been back in England for a week. The Society of Friends might have managed better public relations with the press if they had told the papers of the mission and not, as is implied in Robert Charleton's letter, tried to keep it secret.

The Times printed a half column account on 20th February, mainly taken from a letter from Joseph Sturge to his brother Charles, with an account of waiting for the interview. On Thursday, 23rd February *The Times* quotes from a letter received by Mr. Pease of Darlington from his brother describing the half-hour audience with the Emperor:

> On taking their leave the Emperor shook them heartily by the hand, and on quitting the Palace they were much struck by the cordial reception given to the three plain, humble simple men of peace.

On 28th February *The Times* printed a whole column in very small print, headed *The deputation of the Religious Society of Friends to the Emperor of Russia,* giving a copy of the Address, and the Czar's reply. Other papers also published the Address and the reply.

The Illustrated London News printed a short account: *The Friends and the Czar* in the issue of 4th March and followed this on 11th March with *Peace deputation to the Czar:*

In our last week's number, we recorded the interview which the Deputation from the Society of Friends, (Mr. Joseph Sturge, of Birmingham; Mr. Henry Pease, of Darlington; and Mr. Robert Charleton of Bristol) had with the Emperor of Russia on the 10th ult. This week we engrave a representation of the same, in one of the Cabinets of the Imperial Palace; with Mr. Sturge reading the following Address; to the left of the Emperor is the Baron Nicholay.

For some they had become scapegoats, but their efforts were not ignored.

Letter from Robert Charleton to his wife

RIGA 1 MO 29 1854

My Dearest love,

Agreeably with the plan mentioned in my letter from Konigsberg, we left that town on 5th day night at 10 o'clock and reached Riga 1st evening at 7 – travelling the two days and nights in succession. I was surprised to find on arriving here, how very little we were, either of us, tired by what I should have considered beforehand a very fatiguing operation. The distance from Konigsberg to this place is about 250 miles, and from hence to Petersburg about 400, making a total of 650 miles, instead of 600 as we calculated before. We should not have been so long in coming from Konigsberg, but for a considerable quantity of recently fallen and soft snow towards the Prussian end of the line, which caused us to get along but slowly for a number of hours, but afterwards there was so little snow on the ground, that we have not resorted to the sledge at all, keeping on wheels all the way. We crossed, on the ice, the Niemen at Tilsit, and the Dwina at Riga, both of them broader than the Vistula in addition to several smaller rivers. The weather for the last 2 or 3 days has been unusually mild, seldom many degrees below freezing, and sometimes with a tendency to thaw, though not enough to soften the ground. The cold, before we came here, must have been intense, as we have seen blocks of extremely compact and transparent ice, of 16 inches in thickness. On crossing the Russian frontier a few miles on this side of Tilsit, we were escorted (as is usual) by a horse soldier, a few miles further to the Custom House at Tauroggan, where our luggage was examined by the Russian officials, but not more strictly than is usual

My dearest [Love]

 I arrived with ... ...
from Königsberg, we left that town ... ... at 10 o'clock
& reached Riga last evening at 7 ... the horses ... in
succession — I was surprised ... on arriving here, how ... little
we were, either of us, tired by what ... ... a
very fatiguing ... — The distance from Königsberg to this place is
about 250 miles, & from hence to Petersburg about 400, making a total
of 650 miles, instead of 600, as we calculated before ... ...
been so long in coming from Königsberg, but for a considerable ...
of recently fallen & soft snow ~~on~~ towards the Prussian end of the ... which ...
to get along but slowly for a number of hours ... afterwards ...
so little snow on the ground, that we ... ... the sledge
at all, keeping on wheels all the way — We crossed, on the ice, the Niemen
at Tilsit, & the Dwina at Riga, both of them broader than the ...
in addition to several smaller rivers — The weather ... ... has
has been unusually mild, seldom many degrees below freezing ... sometimes
with a tendency to thaw, though not enough to ... the ground — the
cold, before we came here, must have been intense, to be ... ... block
of extremely compact & transparent ice of 26 inches in thickness ...
crossing the Russian frontier a few miles on this side ... which we were
escorted (as usual) by a horse soldier ...

Letter from Robert Charleton to his wife

at Dover or London. We have found no difficulty whatever in getting along, but have been treated everywhere with great civility and certainly nothing has occured which could in the smallest degree have suggested the idea of the two governments being on bad terms, or likely to go to war. With the exception of some twenty miles, the road in Russia has been extremely good and we have travelled along it as smoothly and as comfortably as we could have done between Bristol and Bath. The country is less dreary than I anticipated, very much of the land being fairly cultivated, and the prospect being agreeably varied by the frequently recurring forests, chiefly of fir and silver birch. The rich dark green of the pine forests contrasts agreeably with the present whiteness of the ground. We travel with 4 active horses harnessed abreast, and when not obstructed by snow, it is easy to make 7 miles an hour. Our carriage proves strong and comfortable, and well adapted for the purpose for which we procured it. The inns, or rather posthouses, on the road afford very little accommodation for travellers; and there is only one place, the University town of Dorpat, between this and Petersburg, where we should be able, with any comfort to stop a night. At all the posthouses, however, they are able to supply boiling water at a short notice; since we entered the Russian territory we have lived principally on the supply of biscuits, tea, etc; which we brought with us; and I suppose we shall continue to do so, after leaving Riga, until we reach Petersburg. Here we are quartered at a pretty comfortable inn, and find the rest agreeable after two days and nights travelling. We are all able to sleep more in the carriage than my former experience of night travelling would have led me to anticipate, and it is doubtless this circumstance, together with our light food which enables us to get on with so little fatigue. When we shall reach Petersburg, depends of course on the state of the road, as to snow, and other circumstances, but we hope to arrive there either on 5th day evening or 6th day.

Afternoon. I wrote all the preceding pretty early this morning. We afterwards sat down and read the scriptures, and held our little meeting. Before dinner we walked out and called on a merchant named Brandt, a business connection of Joseph and Charles Sturge, who gave us some useful information as to the state of the road between this and Petersburg, the result of which is that we shall take a sledge and put our carriage upon it. The weather today is become much colder a sharp frost, and snow falling. We hoped to start tomorrow morning but find that we shall be detained by the passport arrangements, until 10 o'clock. Our friend Brandt informed us that the news from Petersburg is more pacific in its tone, which is of course, gratifying. He also showed us a Berlin paper just received,

34

containing an extract from a London Paper, showing that the object of our mission has been, by some means, divulged. This we were sorry to learn, though probably it was too much to expect the affair could be kept secret. The article was written in a style of harmless drollery, describing us as a mission sent out by the 'Peace Society', that body 'having come to the praiseworthy resolution to save the world; and having it is intimated, provided us for this purpose, with a shipload of Elihu Burritt's Olive Leaves'. We do not ourselves care for this, and do not know that there is any reason to fear that such a premature disclosure of the business may militate against the success of our mission.

A little before dark this afternoon I went out a walk for a mile or so on the Dwina, on which were great numbers of foot passengers and sledges moving along rapidly in various directions. A broad expanse of ice extending up and down the river, as far as the eye can reach, gives one as good an idea of the effect of a frozen sea as anything else well can. Riga is a well built town, though the streets are narrow, with a population of about 10,000. Its prosperity greatly depends on its foreign commerce which is very extensive in Grain, Timber, Tallow, Hemp, and Flax. It is to a very considerable extent a German town, that language being generally spoken as well as the Russian. The upper class of merchants appear to live in a style of great elegance. The suite of apartments into which we were ushered at our friend Brandt's were handsomely furnished as almost any I have seen in England. The mass of people seem to be well employed, and there is a general appearance of thrift and well doing. Many of the inhabitants are Lutherans, and this day of the week is fairly well observed.

I need not say that the prospect of getting a letter from thee as soon as we reach Petersburg, 4 or 5 days hence, is truly pleasant: for though it cannot have been written many days after we parted, the sight of thy hand writing is always welcome, and now more than welcome. With my dear love to our family circle, and also to William and Sarah Tanner, and other friends,

I am thy truly affectionate husband,

Robert Charleton

(PS Written across the first page of this letter)

As we hope if all be well to leave Petersburg not later than tomorrow fortnight, there will not be time for any letter written after this reaches thee, to meet me in that city, and I shall be obliged by thy writing a letter four days after receipt of this to Poste Restante, Riga, and another letter two days later, to the same address, so that whatever may be the time of our leaving Petersburg, either one or both of thy letters may reach me here on the way back, paying the postage at Bristol.

Robert Charleton's message to William and Sarah Tanner was to friends and neighbours who lived at Ashley Farm, near Bristol, and had a special interest and connection with Russia. Sarah Tanner was the eldest daughter of Daniel Wheeler. He and his family had lived in Russia for many years. After Czar Alexander's visit to Westminster Meeting the Czar had asked whether there was a Quaker agriculturalist who was willing to settle in Russia and undertake the drainage and cultivation of derelict crown lands near St. Petersburg. In June 1818, Daniel Wheeler of Sheffield, sailed from Hull with his wife, six children, two other farm workers and their dependents and a tutor for his children. During his fifteen years in Russia he drained thousands of acres of waste and marsh. This improved the health of St. Petersburg with a reduction in fevers and agues which that unhealthy territory bred. But unfortunately his own family suffered. In December 1832 his wife Jane died, while his sons William and Charles and daughter Jane were seriously ill. Jane died in 1837 and was buried beside her mother in a little burial ground near their home. It was these graves which Robert Charleton hoped to be able to visit while he was in Russia, so that he could tell Sarah Tanner about her family burial ground.

Obviously in the middle of winter with the ground covered with deep snow it would have been difficult if not impossible to visit their graves. However, on a later visit to Russia in the summer of 1858 Robert Charleton writes:

There was something indescribably solemn and affecting to the feelings in the sight of the little cemetery at Shoosharry and of the familiar names on the two slabs of granite in that lonely and far off spot. We found everything in good repair and neat order; the railings neatly painted, and the shrubs planted all round grown to a good size. In addition to the two very neat slabs on which are described the names and dates of the deceased alone, there is an upright stone recording the grant of the burying place from the Emperor Nicholas, in Russian characters; and below this in English, the ages of both mother and daughter, the former being described as the wife of Daniel Wheeler. The granite must be of excellent quality as the stone, as well as the inscriptions on them, retain almost their original freshness, not withstanding their exposure to rain and frost; and the material shows scarcely a sign of disintegration.

In 1961, more than a hundred years, two wars and a Revolution later, the graves were again visited by Friends. Richenda Scott accompanied by Fred Tritton went to Leningrad in the hope of tracing the graves, and in her book *Quakers in Russia* writes:

We discovered them by a mixture of luck and persistence lost in the vast distances of the great plain which lies between Leningrad and Dietskoe-Selo. Crossing a wide drainage ditch, surely one of Daniel Wheeler's construction, and thrusting through waist-high soaking grass, we came to a little cemetery holding some 50 or 60 graves, most of them marked by a wooden Russian cross painted a pale blue. The plot was bounded by wooden pailings, and much overgrown by saplings, and almost hidden beneath them stood an upright slab of polished red Finland granite, perhaps five or six feet high, on which was recorded in Russian the gift of the land by the Emperor Nicholas Pavlovitch to the Religious Society of Friends. At right angles to it were two small coffer shaped gravestones of the same red granite, marking the resting place of mother and daughter. The plot lies in the midst of a Soviet experimental farm, established on the land which the Quaker, Daniel Wheeler, had drained and prepared for cultivation 130 years before.

The Burial Ground has been visited recently. In an article in *The Friend* printed in March 1983 Robert Mays and Ken Ward describe how on a visit to the Soviet Union they took the opportunity to find the graves of Jane Wheeler and her daughter at Shushari near Leningrad. They report that:

In acknowledgement of the valuable help given by Daniel Wheeler and his family, the Soviet authorities have now affixed a plaque to the railings surrounding the graves, bearing the following inscription in Russian:

Here lies the wife and daughter of agricultural specialist DANIEL WHEELER an English Quaker. Being in the service of the Russian government together with his sons, William, John and Charles in the period from 1818-1836, he organized the drainage of large areas of land in the region of Ochra Volkova village and Shushari, making them suitable for utilisation and settlement.

The Wheeler grave drawn by Ken Ward shows that the burial ground has been well cared for.

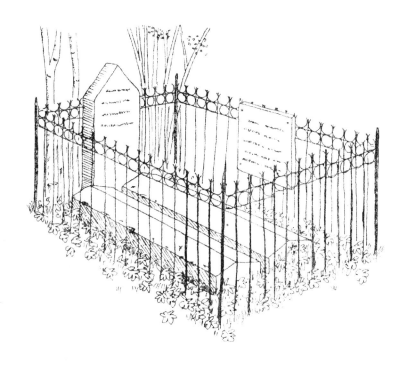

The Grave of Daniel Wheeler and Family

Drawn by Ken Ward

By kind permission of The Friend *& Ken Ward*

CHAPTER IV

Sledge Journey to St. Petersburg

THE LETTERS WRITTEN FROM St. Petersburg on the 2nd and 3rd of February describe their journey, and show that they were relieved to have arrived safely.

They had to present their passports at the frontier post and again at Riga, and register with the police on arrival in St. Petersburg but there seems to have been no difficulty with these formalities. They had had to pay for a 'Padonosha' or power to demand post horses, but the posting system was efficient as they were not held up by a lack of horses, even when they needed extra to pull them through the deep snow drifts. They were fortunate with the weather, and lucky when their carriage overturned not to have been stranded in a snow drift all night, with the risk of hypothermia. They wore fur coats and long fur boots to the knee, which must have made climbing out of the carriage window more difficult, but would have hardly been sufficient protection against the cold which can kill even young marines dressed in the latest 20th-century thermal clothing.

In their letters each writer describes some aspect of the journey which he thinks will be of special interest to his reader. Henry Pease when writing to his fifteen year old son mentions the frozen pig standing up as pigs are wont to do when alive. He admired the horses and drivers, and took one of their caps home with him as a souvenir and hung it on the largest bureau in the library at Pierremont. His daughter Marion in her book *Pierremont Days* says that 'as a child I often wondered what it was, but never remember my father speaking about his journey to Russia'.

Letter from Henry Pease to his son, Henry Fell Pease

ST. PETERSBURG 3 2 MO 54

My dear boy,

Last evening we arrived in this city, thou wilt remember that since thou and I left Darlington it makes fifteen days travel including four or five nights also on the road so that there was not a little satisfaction in entering upon apartments as nicely adapted to our wants as well could be, the additional comfort of letters is not yet mine, but

St. Petersburg

Lithograph in the possession of Lloyd and Grisella Fox

R. Charleton's wife having kindly noticed thy reaching Bristol I have as late an account of thee as I could have, I felt obliged and have requested R.C. to be so kind as to return a message to thee, because beyond a letter to thy dear Grandpa I cannot manage one worth postage by 2.30 when they must leave this house. On 2nd day at Riga I posted a letter to thee. We had to renew our passports there but were not so much detained by this as the slow, slow, slow of the person fixing the carriage on a sledge.

In momentary expectation of it what was there to do but look out of the window into a street more busy than any I have seen in a town of the size say 55,000 – everything on sledges with bells until one's ear was weary. A large proportion of these were laden with merchandise of infinite variety not omitting the frozen pig standing up as pigs are wont to do when alive. I much admired some of the sledges, handsomely built fine horses, capital harness, and portly drivers dressed in well made slate coloured cloaks, with red sash noble high round caps a little raised in the crown, made of dark rich red or blue velvet upon a black velvet forehead piece whilst the rider was dressed in rich furs and a handsome apron of fur.

Soon after two we really started off, and hour after hour patiently worked off six miles including the time lost in changing horses, they are small and for the most part we were obliged to take 6 – ie. 4 abreast and 2 ahead – but as in this country the charge little exceeds a penny-half penny per mile, it is not so very serious a matter. We travelled through the night and proposed to lodge on 3rd day night at Dorpat but got a stage further, we hoped to have done another but the high wind drifted fallen and falling snow so as almost to obliterate the road and bewilder the yamsheik (or driver): at seven a.m. on the 4th day our pilgrimage recommenced, and in twenty four hours ended here. We lost little time with meals, we carried tea, bread with us, at morning and night at post stations, we called for the Samavar (or kettle urn) and having made a light repast, off again. Dinner if it may be so called was discussed as the miles notched off, but even in a sledge progress is not all that could be desired.

Between twelve and one on the fourth day night we suddenly found ourselves on one side at a rather decided angle of incidence. What were we to do? I suppose to get out as quick as possible, what then – how was the carriage to be righted? The yamsheik shouted and flogged, and the English shouted and shouted, and the courier pulled the lead horses, but no! Well yamsheik came to the conclusion that if the carriage would not go up the hill it would go down, so he turned his horses to the open field and having gone say fifty yards left them, walked back to the road the course he would do then fastened on again the little sledge in which we intended to return, and bringing the carriage to the road we started again and went some stages with occasional variety, but rolling over the snow drifts like a ploughed field but more abrupt were jolted in an extra-ordinary manner until we stuck about seven a.m. and had to jump into the snow once more until our horses had got over the worst drifts, and then off again.

Although there has generally been fine snow falling and now is as I write, the accumulation is not great, neither the frost severe, but steady and will continue (or usually does) a month after this. Upon the whole the part of Russia through which we have passed is flat, for a stage or two some undulations and portions very picturesque, but mostly wide and extended bare flats of country, with very few gentlemen's residences, the villages, not attractive, are built of wood same as Norwegian; the forests are very extensive, with but little fine timber, but I cannot tell thee how charming is the effect of these forests of stately pine standing alone on a white carpet – and green branches tipped with snow whilst the forests of silver birch with every twig encrusted, which may be compared to trees of glass – united with all the graceful elegance of which thou canst suppose the birch to admit; these latter (forests of birch) are in places partially with what are called at Darlington, palms, ie. witton blossoms, these having caught a few flakes of snow have peculiar soft pleasing effect.

This being a favourable time for travelling in Russia the one horse sledges are very numerous we meet by twelve to twenty in a string, and see them in greater number drawn up at the bail houses, perhaps the most characteristic sight of this kind was a train of, say, twenty to fifty crossing the lake – it seemed to realise to me so fully pictures of Arctic scenery. Of the inhabitants I can give thee little information, the men seem on an average rather of low stature with occasionally some remarkably fine men; the sheepskin (wool towards the body) is the 'fustian jacket' of this country; I would doubt whether the men wear either linen or cotton next the skin, and they look on 'thick' terms with dirt.

I had on seventh day the pleasure of thy letter (the first from anyone since leaving home) I was much interested in thy details, and approve of thy yielding to thy Uncle's wish to remain with him over second day.

I have been hesitating about sending this off to-day fearing thou wilt deem me slow in writing, but as we are by appointment just going to Count Nesselrodes' office and shall probably learn there whether we are to see the Emperor I will hold another day. We have received several civilities since coming here, to-morrow we dine with an eminent merchant who has also entered our names at a Public Library: another merchant desires us to dine with him, this we have declined for the present. The British Consul has called and subsequently sent us a card of admission to the Hermitage, the object of most interest here. Another family connected with the Imperial household requests a morning call, this we have declined.

On our journey the cold was not severe, but it is now sharp enough here 6 degrees above zero and a steady breeze, the air full of fine icy pines glittering in the brilliant sunshine. We have had a long walk to see the frozen market, fish, flesh and fowl all hard as stone and only to be cut up by the aid of mallets, then through the Neveski, the principal street of the city one and a half miles long, we passed an extraordinary number of public buildings, also the justly celebrated Statue of Peter the Great, but nothing in art could compare with the beauty of the ice-covered trees glittering in the sun and looking through them a pure blue sky above. Thou would greatly admire the sledge horses in what style they dash along making the fine snow fly like dust.

2nd day 2-15 just returned from a most polite interview with Count Nesselrode who states that the Emperor will make an appointment to receive the Address and on our enquiry said it was probable the Heir Apparent would be present.

Write to me by the early post. Post say by 4th or 5th day with Poste Restante Berlin.

Thy very affectionate father,

H. Pease

The Quaker delegation were very fortunate to have an introduction to W. C. Gellibrand, a most knowledgeable Englishman, who had been a resident in Russia for many years. He was able to give them information about the Russian Court and government. He advised them that they should write direct to Count Nesselrode, the Russian Chancellor, asking for permission to present the Address to Czar Nicholas. They stressed that they were a religious mission and not a political one, so that they did not want to involve the British Embassy. For this reason they did not call on the British Ambassador until after they had seen the Czar. It must have been encouraging for them that W. C. Gellibrand thought that their undertaking was well-timed and not too late to be useful.

The diplomatic situation was complicated. On 23rd January, while the Quaker deputation was travelling from Dusseldorf to Berlin, the British

Foreign Secretary, Lord Clarendon, received Baron Brunnow, the Russian Ambassador in London, and considered Count Nesselrode's inquiry as to whether the allies meant to keep Turkey from attacking Russia. Count Nesselrode's instructions to Brunnow had been that if a satisfactory answer to his inquiry was not given by Clarendon, diplomatic relations were to be broken off. On 31st January, Clarendon gave Brunnow what was to prove an unsatisfactory answer. The court at St. Petersburg did not yet know that, and it appears that Brunnow did not immediately upon receipt of Clarendon's reply, send a courier off to Nesselrode. Rather he waited a few days before acting. This delay was most fortunate for the Quaker delegation, as the great question in St. Petersburg diplomatic circles at the moment the deputation arrived was 'what was Clarendon's stance and how would Brunnow respond to it?' Obviously the three Quakers had no idea of these developments.

For the information on the diplomatic situation I am indebted to Stephen Frick's article *The Quaker Deputation to Russia: Foreign Office British and Foreign State paper 1853-54 Vol XLIV p98-105 'Correspondence respecting the suspension of diplomatic relations between Great Britain and Russia, January and February 1854'*.

Letter from Robert Charleton to his wife

PETERSBURG SECOND MONTH 2

We were favoured to arrive here in safety about seven o'clock this evening; and it ought to excite, and, I trust it does excite, feelings of thankfulness that we should have been permitted to perform a journey of such length, and under such circumstances, in so safe and agreeable a manner. We are in very comfortable quarters at Benson's Hotel, and since tea we have had some serious conversation as to the best mode of setting about the very important business which has brought us here; and which we intend cautiously proceeding with as soon as we hear from the post.

We left Riga at two o'clock on Second day afternoon, and slept at Iggafer, a post station on the road, on Third day night; but, with this exception, and a short time for meals, we travelled on, without stopping, until we arrived here. The thermometer, I believe, never quite down to 20 Fahrenheit; which is very mild indeed, compared with what it had been before our arrival here. Our carriage was put on a sledge at Riga, and we have travelled in this way ever since. On some part of the road there was a considerable thickness of imperfectly frozen snow, which made it heavy work to drag the sledge through; and had our carriage been on wheels, it would have been very difficult to proceed at all; as it was we were obliged to have six horses most of the way from Riga. The road for some miles skirted along the shores of Lake Peipus, a large expanse of water, now of course ice, about fifty or sixty miles long, and thirty or forty miles wide. We passed over this part of the road in the day time, and the sight of a long train of sledges crossing over the lake in a different direction, a long way from the shore, combined with the heavy drifts of snow blown up like sand hills on the coast, gave to the scene a peculiarly arctic character. In order to prevent the formation of snow drifts on the road, a sort of fence parallel to it is made with fir boughs stuck into the ground, which has the effect of checking the progress of the driving snow, and causing it to accumulate in a thick bed along the line of the fence, but not reaching the road itself. A similar effect we saw produced in one or two places by a rough wall, instead of a fir hedge, made of blocks of frozen snow. This precaution is not needed when the road passes through forests, but only when the country is open. In one place, where this precaution was neglected, there were drifts of snow in the road, making it as uneven as the swell of the sea, and imparting to the sledge a similar motion. Once our carriage was stuck in a hollow between two drifts, and we were obliged to alight before the horses could pull it out.

We met with quite a little adventure during last night. Our driver in passing some other sledges, got too near the side of the road, so our carriage slipped sideways part of the way down a sloping bank, and seemed within the merest trifle of turning over. We got out on the upper side, and made some ineffectual attempts to replace the sledge on the road; but, when we were becoming a little alarmed at the idea of passing the night in so inhospitable a spot, the driver, urging the horses, dexterously drew the sledge, without upsetting down the remainder of the bank into an open space below, and to the distance of some twenty or thirty yards from the foot of the bank; and then turning the horses round, he forced them into a gallop towards the bank, and, with the momentum thus acquired, drew the sledge, with the carriage on it, up the bank into the road again. Happily there was no material damage done to the carriage, and in a quarter of an hour we were again seated in it, proceeding on our way as if nothing had occurred. We felt that there was cause for much thankfulness that we should have been so preserved, for it would have been very unpleasant, if not injurious, to us to have been detained all night on the snow by the upset carriage.

The villages between this and Riga are all built of wood, like the American log-houses, but more neatly finished, many of them,

45

indeed, with all the neatness of a Swiss cottage whilst the poorer ones are constructed with the unsquared pine logs, the interstices between the logs being stuffed with moss, which must make them warm and comfortable. The peasants are generally dressed in loose garments, of rough woollens or sheepskins with the wool turned inside. They appear well fed, and it is humiliating to think how much better condition are the peasantry of this rude country, than the corresponding class of our own fellow subjects in Ireland.

Our journey has been performed without the slightest impediment from political causes. Indeed, it is difficult to reconcile the entire freedom with which we have passed along; our passports not having been once looked at during the four hundred miles from Riga; with the accounts current in England of the continual and vexatious interference of Government officials in Russia.

Our hotel is on the south bank of the Neva, a noble river, about twice as wide as the Thames at London, which we cross on the ice to our friend W. C. Gellibrand's, who lives on the quay on the opposite side. Petersburg is a splendid city, judging at least from the little we have seen of it.

Robert Charleton

Letter from Robert Charleton to Samuel Fox

PETERSBURG 2ND MONTH 3RD 1854

My dear Uncle,

Thou wilt doubtless have heard through the notes to Joseph Cooper by Joseph Sturge and myself of our arrival successively at Berlin, Konigsberg, and Riga; but thy deep interest in the object of our mission, and thy own and Aunt's very great kindness and hospitality to my dear wife and myself personally, make me unwilling to delay writing to inform thee of our safe arrival here last evening after a journey performed with more facility and less fatigue than I could have at all expected. We came from Konigsberg to Riga on wheels, but from Riga to this place our carriage was placed on a sledge, the state of the roads making that the most advantageous mode of travelling.

We called this morning on W. C. Gellibrand, and had a long conversation with him on the subject of our mission. He entirely sympathises with it, and has given us some valuable advice as to the

46

best mode of carrying it into effect. We were much encouraged to find that he thinks our undertaking well timed, and by no means too late to be useful. We are to take tea with him this evening, when arrangements will be made for making a beginning. We feel the need for caution and watchfulness, lest through inadvertence or eagerness to get on, we should in any way damage the object of the Meeting for Sufferings; but we hope to proceed with as much despatch as is consistent with this caution. We generally avoid conversation on political subjects, but from what we have seen and heard, it is certain that there is no such general enthusiasm in favour of war, as has been present in England. I believe on the contrary there is a strong and general desire for the preservation of peace; in the Baltic provinces certainly. We find that the mere anticipation of war has already had a most unjurious influence on Russian Commerce, the price of foreign manufactures and merchandise having much advanced, whilst native produce has proportionately fallen, and we hear of trade in many districts almost paralysed, and money becoming very scarce. Joseph Sturge and Henry Pease as well as myself are favoured to be in good health, and unite with me in love to thyself and our other dear friends who were so kindly interested in our welfare. I am this morning in receipt of a letter from my dear Catherine, with a satisfactory account of herself and all at home, which is a favour for which I desire to be truly thankful. I feel also that gratitude is due, in no small degree, for the favour that has been shown us in being permitted to accomplish our long journey, undertaken under such peculiar circumstances, not only in safety but without any material interruption or drawback from any cause.

With dear love to Aunt and thyself

I am thy affectionate nephew,

Robert Charleton

Robert Charleton and Henry Pease comment on the appearance of the villages and the peasants who lived in them. They were surprised that the condition of the peasantry in Russia seemed much better than in Ireland, a country which they had both visited, and which was suffering from the terrible effects of the potato famine and evictions.

All the writers were pleased that they had not been delayed by any interference from Government officials. In fact their journey to St. Petersburg had been easier than any of them had dared to hope.

Joseph Sturge's letters from St. Petersburg give more details of the journey.

Letter from Joseph Sturge

PETERSBURG 2ND MO 2 1854

Although, as thou mayst suppose, somewhat wearied with our journey, I wish just to commence a letter to say we arrived here about seven o'clock this evening, and are located at Miss Benson's, on the English quay, as comfortably as we could have been at almost any hotel in England. We are all in good health, and got on far better than, from the state of the roads, we could have anticipated, and have met with as much civility and attention as if we had been subjects of the Emperor of Russia himself. As we had mostly to employ six, and on one occasion seven horses, from the heavy drifts of snow in some parts of the road, we calculate we have had the help of upwards of 200 Russian horses to bring us here, at the low charge of about three half-pence per mile for each horse, and we have reason to be thankful so far that we have not met with any mishap worth notice. We have come with our carriage on a sledge all the way from Riga, and the latter has proved so strong, and the former so secured to it, as to stand, without any material injury, all the shocks of our journey.

Letter from Joseph Sturge

PETERSBURG 2ND MO 4 1854

I wrote by last post, briefly mentioning our arrival here. We were detained in Riga nearly four hours longer than we intended, in consequence of the breaking of a part of our travelling apparatus in fixing the carriage to the sledge, and which in England would probably have been put right in half-an-hour, so that we did not leave Riga until two o'clock in the afternoon. We went to the government office in that city by appointment at ten o'clock, where our passports were exchanged for another document, which among other things described our persons, and also contained instructions in English, of how we were to proceed on our arrival in Petersburg.

The number of conveyances in Riga, principally sledges, many of them elegantly fitted up, far exceeds anything I had seen in any city of the size before. In the street opposite our hotel, it was often as crowded as Cheapside, and as each owner of a sledge is obliged to have one or more bells on his horse or horses, there was a continual jingle not only in the day but through the night. It seems singular that in this cold climate almost all the middle classes ride even short distances, and the ladies in an open drosky, with apparently as little covering as they use in walking in England, while the gentlemen not only ride but walk in their fur coats.

After we had proceeded two stages with four horses, during which the snow continued to fall, we had to take six horses; and towards eleven o'clock it fell so heavily that even our courier began to think it might be safest to stop at the next posting station for fear of being blocked up in the road. However, towards midnight it abated, and with an extra horse one stage we got through the night; and the following day with six horses, we travelled at the rate of from six to eight miles an hour, losing from fifteen to forty minutes at the different stations, which are at the average distance of about twenty Russian versts, or about fourteen miles. We were agreeably surprised to find these stations, instead of being worse, much better than before we arrived at Riga. They are handsomely built, and well furnished, and it is part of the regulations that the occupiers should keep them well heated with stoves during the winter. The house, firewood, and furniture are provided by the government, and a part of the latter seems to be one or more pictures of the Emperor. The rooms for visitors seem generally well cleaned, but we soon had proof that it was not always the case with parts more out of sight!

We arrived at Dorpat, where there is a University of about 600 students, about seven o'clock the second evening, and, thinking it would divide the distance better to Petersburg, we proceeded to the next posting station, and found the sleeping accommodation really cleaner and better than the hotel at Riga. We started between six and seven in the morning, and during a good part of the day passed along the north shore of Lake Piepus, which was often in sight, but which was for the most part enveloped in mist; in one place, however, we could see, I should suppose, not less than a hundred sledges passing along it, as being in some places nearer as well as smoother than the road. The number of small sledges with one horse is great in this part of Russia. Sledges being the principal, and in winter the only means of transit for all kinds of produce and merchandise, we met or passed them at all hours of the night as well as day. Generally a considerable number of them go together, and there are large sheds on the road, not far from the posting stations, in which the men and their horses can get under cover. While on the banks of the Piepus we were not unfrequently to pass through some rather deep drifts of fresh-fallen snow, and I was surprised to see how well six little horses, with our heavy sledge behind them, would pull through it, and come in comparatively fresh at the end of the stage, when English horses would probably be knocked up with even a light weight behind them.

Our plan with meals has been to take our breakfast and tea at the posting houses, where they find us good water and good milk, and use our own tea, coffee, cocoa, and biscuits, raisins, and an apple to which we added in Riga a tongue, a bit of beef, a little butter, and a little jar of preserve, which lasted us to Petersburg.

11 o'clock p.m. We are just returned from a visit to W. C. Gellibrand, who gave us some private details of deep interest of the Royal Family of Russia, which, coming from an intelligent Christian Englishman who has resided here forty years with unusual means of information, may I think be relied upon, and which places the character of the present Emperor in a more favourable light than we have been wont to view it in England; but I must defer writing more at present, further than saying that we have prepared a note to Count Nesselrode, and W. C. Gellibrand has engaged to send it to him at ten o'clock tomorrow morning.

CHAPTER V

Waiting and Wondering

THERE ARE SEVERAL interesting letters written from St. Petersburg while the delegation were waiting and wondering whether they would be able to see the Czar. These letters show that they were anxious to proceed cautiously and not to do anything which might prejudice their chances of an interview with the Emperor. They at first declined Count Nesselrode's offer of a guide to show them some of the interesting sights of the city: but after they had had a cordial reception by the Count they decided to accept the offer of a guided tour of 'The Hermitage', one of the most famous art galleries in the world. They also visited some other places of interest in St. Petersburg. It might have seemed rude to the Russians if they had not agreed to do some sightseeing while they were waiting.

An extract from a letter written by Joseph Sturge gives some insight into his feelings, and the difficulty which they faced in refusing invitations without appearing discourteous:

> Count Nesselrode has requested his private secretary to accompany us to see the most remarkable sights in the city, but I must confess that my mind is too ill at ease with the prospect of the visit to the Emperor before us on which so much may depend, and at which it may be so important not to say too little or too much, to enjoy the most interesting sights, even if I had not outlived my curiosity in respect to such matters. But as Count Nesselrode, who is Chancellor of the Empire, the highest office of the state, had especially appointed this gentleman to show us anything we might like to see, it would have been discourteous to refuse.

> We have been today to what is called 'The Hermitage', which is attached to the Winter Palace, where the Emperor and his family now reside, though it does not actually form part of it. We have spent about three hours there, and as Henry Pease observed when we left, if we could describe the beauty and magnificence of the place, which it would be scarcely possible to do, our friends would consider it an exaggeration. Of course we could only take a cursory view, though we probably walked a mile or more through galleries and rooms fitted up in the most costly and at the same time most chaste style. Some are devoted to medals and coins chiefly of gold and silver, and arranged according to the different countries to which they belong; others to

statues ancient and modern; but the greater proportion to pictures, different rooms being set apart for the artists of different nations. But what perhaps strikes most is the costly character of the furniture of the different suites of rooms, the richness and highly polished finish of the multitude of Italian marble pillars, generally of one single block, the beauty of the ceilings etc.

We are becoming rather unpleasantly objects of curiosity, and as it will get out that the Chancellor has received us cordially and the Emperor has determined to receive the Address, we shall become more so, and we shall be anxious to get out of the way as soon as we possibly can. We already find it difficult to refuse invitations without appearing uncourteous, though we have delivered scarcely any of our letters of introduction. We have consented to dine with A. Mirrilies, a friend of W. C. Gellibrand, tomorrow evening, and we are intending to go to see a school in which he is much interested tomorrow morning.

I find the English gentlemen, and especially the ladies, have admitted pretty strongly anti-Russian feelings, and except where there is a very strong interest in favour of peace, I fear that they would not be sorry to see England at war with this country; and if they say as much to the Russians as they do among themselves, it is not surprising that there should be, as they allege there is, an increasing anti-British feeling among the Russians. All parties, however, admit that the Emperor has qualities of private character which we in England do not give him credit for; that he is not only kind but affectionate in the private and domestic relations of life, and it is said on pretty good authority that he devotes nearly an hour daily to his private devotions.

Letter from Robert Charleton to his wife, Catherine

PETERSBURG 2ND MONTH 4TH DAY 1854

My dearest love

I necessarily finished my letter of yesterday with so much haste I have scarcely time to say how much I value and appreciate the expressions of sympathy and affection contained in thy letter of the 24th and how very cordial to me was the appearance which however I did not need of thy often commending me to the shepherd of Israel. I often think of thee in the midst of our various journeyings and indulge myself in looking forward to the time when through the divine favour

52

we may be permitted to meet again. We took tea 1st evening at W. C. Gellibrand's and found him a most intelligent and interesting character. The time was spent in instructive conversation; the information which he gave us with regard to Russia and Russian concerns, being such as it would have been scarcely possible to get from books. Considering that the object of our mission is doubtless well known to the Russian authorities, it having come to his notice through the public papers before our arrival, he recommended us to take the direct course of addressing a letter to Count Nesselrode explaining the object of our visit, and proposing an interview with him for further explanation, preparatory to presenting the Address. On reflection, we entirely agreed in the wisdom of this course, and addressed a letter accordingly to Count Nesselrode who has today favoured us with a prompt reply appointing 2nd day at 1 o'clock for us to see him at the Foreign Ministry. He politely sent a special messenger to our hotel offering his services in showing us any objects of interest in St. Petersburg. We acknowledged his kindness, but declined for the present to avail ourselves of it; intimating however that we might perhaps be glad to do so when the main object of our journey is accomplished. Thou will thus see that up to this point matters were of promising appearance and I only hope that we may be preserved from doing harm by any inadventure or want of prudence on our part. We were engaged for about two hours this morning visiting the British Consul's Office, the Alien Office, and the Secret Police Office in order to comply with the formalities which must be observed by foreigners coming into Russia; but the very superficial character of our examination by the Government functionaries makes it almost certain they must have received instructions from higher quarters not to obstruct our proceedings.

The weather has become much colder, my thermometer this morning at 8 o'clock outside the window being at 15 degrees. This is considered mild for Russia, and it is certainly not unpleasant to our feelings. But whatever the temperature outside, the temperature indoors is kept so agreeably warm by the porcelain stoves so that it is quite common to see greenhouse plants thriving abundantly in it. Mr. Gellibrand's drawing room last evening was delightfully perfumed with the fragrance of hyacinths in blossom and even in the post houses in the country we have seen various kinds of geraniums, and even orange and other delicate shrubs. Whilst transacting our business this morning we saw a good deal of the finest part of Petersburg. The public buildings are extremely splendid, and the streets wide and well built; altogether it has the air of a very magnificent but not very commercial city. I am today in receipt of a message from thee my dearest through a letter to Henry Pease from his father from which I am glad to learn that thou has received my letter from Dusseldorf.

Second day morning. The above was written on seventh day. We yesterday held a little meeting as usual the day being spent quietly at our quarters with the exception of going out a little for exercise. The British Consul kindly called on us, politely offering his services in any way that he could be of use to us. The weather continued to grow colder and we may very likely have a taste of real Russian winter before we leave. The thermometer was steady at 13 or 14 degrees through the whole of yesterday and this morning it is falling to 9 or 23 degrees below the freezing point. In a Northern aspect it stands as low as 5 and a half or 6 degrees. As we are to see Count Nesselrode at one o'clock today we shall most probably not be returned in time to send letters for todays post afterwards; and I therefore mean to send this before we go there. We hope it may be arranged for us to see the Emperor not later than tomorrow or next day though it must be as yet uncertain whether he will see us, especially as he has been unwell and confined to the house for some days. Should we succeed without much delay in accomplishing the object of our visit we hope to leave Petersburg on 6th day to spend next 1st day at Dorpat, more than half way to Riga. Next 1st day week at Berlin and to reach home during that week say the 5th or 6th day, the 23rd or 24th. These arrangements must however as yet be regarded as conditional and it is quite possible that we may not reach home for a few days after the time indicated, but I propose writing again before we leave Petersburg. Hoping to get another letter from thee in the course of a few days as arranged before I left home and to receive further intelligence at Riga and Berlin.

I am thy very affectionate husband,

Robert Charleton

My dear love to Father and Anna and to our other relations and friends as usual. Since we have been here we have not seen the smallest appearance of any enthusiasm or popular feeling in favour of war, very much the contrary. I believe there is a strong and general desire for the preservation of peace. The mere apprehension of war has had the effect of paralysing commerce to a very much greater extent here than in England. A very large proportion of the staple trade of Russia, tallow, timber, flax, hemp etc. is carried on by means of British capital the gradual withdrawal of which is already occasioning no little distress among the smaller class of dealers as well as the producers in the interior. Foreign goods are all very considerably advanced, whilst the native produce of Russia is proportionally declining in price. We hear for instance of flax having fallen 20% or even lower within the last two or three months in consequence of the absence of the usual purchases for spring delivery.

Letter from Robert Charleton to his wife, Catherine

PETERSBURG 2ND MONTH 6TH DAY 1854

My dearest love,

My letter today was sent to the post just before our visit to Count Nesselrode. He had appointed to see us at one but sent us word that in consequence of having business with the Emperor he wished our interview postponed until half-past-one. That he should thus send purposely to avoid keeping us waiting half-an-hour we thought a rather unusual mark of politeness. At the appointed hour we went and after being shown through a long suite of rooms, in which were stationed a number of officials, in and out of livery, we were ushered into the Count's private apartment, where he received us with great courtesy and affability. Joseph Sturge read the Address to him, and some remarks were added. Count Nesselrode expressed his entire concurrence in the sentiments contained in the Address, and his appreciation of the motives by which it was dictated. He said that the Emperor who has been apprised of our arrival, would be quite willing to allow us to present the Address at a private interview, and that we should be informed as soon as a suitable time could be fixed. We referred to the intercourse with the late Emperor Alexander of our Friends William Allen and Thomas Shillitoe, and he himself added a reference to Daniel Wheeler. We have no reason to doubt the entire sincerity of the Count's expressions of satisfaction with our visit, as we are informed on good authority that he is personally very much opposed to the war.

We feel it the cause for thankfulness that our work should thus far have proceeded satisfactorily; and we have only to wait patiently until we get the summons to wait on the Emperor. We hope that under no circumstances will our visit here have done harm. It seems at all events to have excited a good deal of observation, and we have had various calls and invitations to dinner both from the English residents and foreigners; but, for the present we think it best to decline these invitations excepting that we are going tomorrow to dine at W. C. Gellibrand's.

55

We have today done a little sightseeing. We visited the Frozen Market. The carcasses of cattle and pigs as well as the poultry and fish in a state of perfect rigidity present a singular and somewhat repulsive appearance. As the frozen flesh and the bone are of nearly the same degree of hardness the art of the butcher is extremely simple. Instead of dividing the pig into joints the animal is sawn or chopped through in straight cuts, from back to belly like the slices of a jam roll. The saw or chopper passing alike through bone and flesh without any regard to anatomical structure. It was curious to see a large fish like a cod divided by the fishmonger into pieces for sale, the man holding a knife across the back of the fish and forcing it through by blows with a wooden hammer the knife penetrating into the fish perhaps a quarter or half an inch with each blow.

We also rode out in a sledge about ten miles down the Gulf Finland half way to Kronstadt keeping almost to the middle of the Gulf. But instead of gliding smoothly over the ice, we found it more uneven and jolting than travelling on the land. The ice is covered with snow several feet in thickness, which owing to the great traffic to and from Kronstadt is worked into ruts quite as deep and irregular as those in a muddy lane in winter. I think the motion made me feel squeamish, not altogether unlike being seasick. There is a line of posts or long poles driven into the ice to indicate the proper course, with stations or wooden houses, like watch boxes, at short intervals from which a light is hoisted at night, and where in foggy weather or during a snow storm, a bell is kept constantly ringing. These precautions are highly needful, for a heavy fall of snow would soon obliterate the track, and the shore not being visible on either side, under such circumstances a sledge would soon be lost, and the travellers in danger of being frozen. The thermometer has not risen above 9 or 10 degrees all day and there being considerable wind, made it feel very cold; but I have not taken cold, and neither of us are at all the worse for the exposure although the sledge was by no means so warm as our travelling carriage.

3rd day morning.

It is milder than yesterday, the thermometer being 4 or 5 degrees higher. We do not like to go far from home thinking it uncertain how soon we may be summoned to see the Emperor but if we don't hear before we intend going out in the afternoon to do a little shopping. W. C. Gellibrand and another English merchant have called on us this morning. The Queen's speech has been received here by telegraph as far as Konigsberg and as far as we can learn is not unfavourably interpreted by the merchants.

4th day morning.

As we received yesterday no communication from the Palace I fear there is no prospect of seeing the Emperor today and we may perhaps be still kept waiting some days so I think it is certain that we shall not return so early as the time hinted at in my last letter. All we can do is to exercise patience in the matter and considering how closely the Emperor's time is occupied with important business, and that his health has not been good lately, we must not regard it as a hardship to have to wait. We yesterday afternoon bought some prints with views of Petersburg etc. and a few other little matters as remembrances of our being in Russia, and afterwards went to dine at W. C. Gellibrand's who received us with the greatest hospitality and kindness having invited a party of English and American friends to meet us with whom the evening was pleasantly passed in conversation.

We are to be escorted this morning by one of Count Nesselrode's private secretaries to some of the public institutions here. This will doubtless be interesting but we shall feel our minds more free to derive enjoyment from such sources when our main business is got through, but as Count Nesselrode has twice offered us this kind attention we did not think it would be courteous to decline it.

At W. C. Gellibrand's we saw the Queen's speech in print in Gaglinaius paper of the 1st February. This paper which is printed in English in Paris is more taken by the English here than any paper from England. All foreign newspapers sent to Russia are revised by the censor and passages considered objectionable are cut out or blotted out. It sometimes happens, that so much is cut away that the remainder will hardly hold together.

Mary Gellibrand was much interested in hearing such particulars as I gave them respecting our dear friends William and Sarah Tanner, W. C. Gellibrand observed that the part of the land which was formally occupied by the Wheeler family is so much altered and built over that he could with difficulty recognise the entrance to the place, the last time he was passing that way. Should we have the opportunity of readily doing it we intend going to the burial place as proposed by Sarah Tanner, but it will scarcely be worth while delaying our departure a day or omitting anything else of much importance on this account as the ground is covered with snow of such thickness that it is doubtful if we should be able to identify the spot, and certainly not to make any accurate report of it's condition, yet I hope not withstanding we shall go there. Please mention this to Sarah Tanner with my dear love. The thermometer is again today down to 6 degrees or 26 degrees below freezing but there being no wind it does not feel nearly so cold as two days ago.

Since writing the above we have been with Count Nesselrode's secretary over the new Palace called the Hermitage. Such a profusion of works of art, including marbles, paintings, statuary, etc. but, more especially the splendour and costlyness of the building itself, we were totally unprepared for. We spent about two hours in making a very cursory and superficial visit to this wonderful place. The authorities were exceedingly polite and courteous showing us some parts of the building not usually exhibited to strangers. Henry Pease remarked that the profusion of gold reminded him of the description of Solomon's making that precious metal plentiful in Jerusalem. There is one room in the Palace appropriated to coins and medals of different countries. Among them was a series of the coins of England from Ethelred down to Victoria embracing all the changes in a period of over a thousand years. We are to be conducted tomorrow by the same gentleman to some other objects of interest though as a matter of choice we should prefer completing the object of our mission to any amount of lionising.

P.S. 4th day afternoon, 2nd month, 1854.

I am today in receipt of thy letter the 30th ult. It is indeed truly welcome. I desire to feel thankful for the cheering report thou art able to give both of thyself and of matters of home. I am glad to find thou was going to Wellington to visit Thomas. Give him my dear love and also thank Father and Anna for their kind care in visiting Kingswood and Oldland Common during my absence. I am pleased to hear a favourable report of these two establishments, and am interested in finding thou has been employed in exchanging the books and china between Cotham and Ashley Down. It is satisfactory to have got through John Wilber's visit so harmlessly.

I fear there is little prospect of seeing the Emperor tomorrow and if so we shall certainly not leave Petersburg this week. I hope to write again about 7th day and will with very much love and warm appreciation of the affection and tenderness in thy truly valuable letter.

I am thy ever affectionate husband,

Robert Charleton

Please give my love to Thomas Tanner with my best thanks for his kind attention with regard to the lectures at Bedminster and also let him know how we are getting on.

Robert Charleton's references to Kingswood and Oldland Common were to the schools which he had founded in Bristol. His interest in education is further illustrated in his next letter when he writes that they had been shown round the Lancastrian school for foreign children in St. Petersburg. The Lancastrian system of education was founded by a Quaker, Joseph Lancaster, at the end of the 18th century. He made experiments in teaching and adopted the monitorial system, where the older children taught the younger ones.

William Allen in describing his first meeting with Joseph Lancaster wrote:

I can never forget the impression which the scene made on me. Here I beheld a thousand children collected from the streets, where they were learning nothing but mischief one boy corrupting another, all reduced to the most perfect order, and training to habits of subordination and usefulness, and learning the great truths of the gospel from the Bible.

The Duke of Bedford was one of Joseph Lancaster's earliest patrons. He obtained an audience for him with George III, who is supposed to have said, 'I wish that every poor child in my dominions may be able to read his Bible'. The royal favour helped the spread of the Lancastrian schools system of mutual or monitorial instruction, which was established not only in England but in most parts of the civilised world, including Russia.

Letter from Robert Charleton to his wife, Catherine

PETERSBURG 2ND MONTH 9TH 1854

My dearest love,

My letter of yesterdays date will have informed thee of our interview with Count Nesselrode and various other particulars. Count Nesselrode's private secretary called on us again today and showed us over a public building called the 'Mining Corps' containing a very interesting collection of mineralogical specimens and also models of coal and silver mines in Siberia showing the various operations connected with the production of those metals. There is also a full size model of the enormous mammoth skeleton found embedded in the ice some years ago, compared with which an elephant would look quite small. Nothing can exceed the kind attention that has been shown to us by the gentlemen connected with these institutions, but what is of greater immediate importance to us is that Count Nesselrode's secretary thinks it probable, though not yet certain, that we shall be admitted to see the Emperor tomorrow.

At an earlier hour this morning we were conducted by A. Mirrilies to the Lancastrian School here, established chiefly for the children of Germans and other foreigners. It has now been in existence twenty-nine years, and appears to have been very useful to great numbers of the poor of this class. There were nearly three hundred children present when we called, and we heard them read both German and Russian. We were a good deal interested with our visit, though we could not understand what we heard, excepting through my own imperfect knowledge of German. We also went to see the Ice Hills, which is a very favourite amusement, resorted to for exercise and pleasure by numbers of the English here. I spoke to W. C. Gellibrand today about visiting the Wheelers' cemetery. He offered to go with me there if I decidedly wished it but thought that no purpose would be answered at present on account of the snow, but said he would make a point of going there himself before coming to England this summer, and would take care to give the necessary instructions to have the railings etc. neatly kept up. We are going to dinner this evening at A. Mirrilies. This gentleman has shown us much kind attention. He has resided here twenty-eight years and is one of the parties mentioned to us by John Venning of Norwich.

Evening. We have dined and taken tea at A. Mirrilies where we met a party of friends kindly invited to meet us consisting mostly of the same persons we met on third day at W. C. Gellibrand's, including of course W. C. G. and wife.

Whilst at A. Mirrilies we received a communication from Count Nesselrode informing us that it is appointed,for us to see the Emperor tomorrow at half-past-one. We strongly feel the importance and responsibility of our position at this moment and the great need we have for the guidance of a wisdom better than our own, at so critical a juncture. The news from England today is considered extremely unfavourable; and there seems to be a general impression here, growing in strength, that war will not be avoided. If, under these circumstances the feeble instrumentality of our mission should be permitted to assist, in ever so slight a degree, in turning the scale in favour of peace, it would indeed, be cause for humble thankfulness. The English residents here who know most about it represent the character of the Emperor as very different from what we have so often heard it stated to be in England. In the relations of domestic life, he is said to be most exemplary; and so devoted to the interests of his subjects as to be almost idolized by them. Strange, too, as it may seem to us, who have long been accustomed to hear the contrary, he is believed by the best informed English here, to be acting in the present Turkish quarrel from a real sense of duty, and from a sincere belief, however mistaken, that he is in the right. This being the case, I am very glad the Meeting for Sufferings adopted the strain of Address which characterises the document we have to present tomorrow. I believe that nothing could be so well adapted to the circumstances of the case. W. C. Gellibrand, who enters most kindly into our position and feelings, says that, while feeling the solemnity of our present engagement, he considers that the probability of such a mission being useful now, is a hundred times greater than it would have been several months ago, or at any former period of the dispute. Without attaching too much weight to such an opinion it is very satisfactory to find the judgement of the Meeting for Sufferings so strongly confirmed by a person, so well informed, and so well able to judge as W. C. Gellibrand.

6th day morning.

After writing the foregoing last evening I had an attack of diarrhoea. I don't know whether it was the result of drinking the Neva water which is said to have this tendency, or some fruit we partook of at A. Mirrilies or whether a reaction from the opposite of the system a week or ten days ago but it hindered me from sleeping and I feel this morning languid and flat with some feverishness but the diarrhoea is stopped and I quite hope that by a good nights rest to be well as usual tomorrow morning, but for the moment I feel my condition the very reverse of what one would have liked for going to the Palace. Happily however J. Sturge and H. Pease are both quite up to par.

6th day afternoon.

We have had an interview with the Emperor. He received us with great kindness and gave us a full opportunity to not only read him the Address, which was done by Joseph Sturge, but of adding such remarks as we agreed beforehand to be desirable, and which was done likewise chiefly by J. Sturge. We were with him nearly half an hour and were afterwards invited to see the Empress and her daughter the Grand Duchess of Leuchtenberg in another apartment. It would be altogether impossible for me, in this note, to relate the substance of what passed but we shall endeavour to put down as much as we can recollect before the impression fades from our memory. On the whole I think we have great reason to be thankful that this engagement arduous as it was in prospect, has been so comfortably got through and I trust at least no harm has been done. We shall in all probability leave Petersburg on 2nd day but intend writing once again before we leave, and in great haste in order to save a post.

I am thy very affectionate husband,
Robert Charleton

P.S. I am already feeling better and hope tomorrow to be as well as usual.

Robert Charleton

CHAPTER VI

Visit to the Czar

THE ADDRESS FROM THE Society of Friends which Joseph Sturge read and presented to the Czar was worded thus:

To Nicholas, Emperor of all the Russias.

May it please the Emperor.

We, the undersigned, members of a meeting representing the religious Society of Friends, commonly called Quakers in Great Britain, venture to approach the Imperial presence, under a deep conviction of religious duty, and in the constraining love of Christ our Saviour.

We are, moreover, encouraged so to do by the many proofs of condescension and Christian kindness manifested by thy late illustrious brother, the Emperor Alexander, as well as by thy honoured Mother, to some of our brethren in religious profession.

It is well known that, apart from all political consideration, we have, as a Christian Church, uniformly upheld a testimony against war, on the simple ground that it is utterly condemned by the precepts of Christianity, as well as altogether incompatible with the Spirit of it's Divine Founder, who is emphatically styled the 'Prince of Peace'. This conviction we have repeatedly pressed upon our own rulers, and in language of bold but respectful remonstrance, we have urged upon them the maintenance of peace, as the true policy as well as the manifest duty of a Christian Government.

And now, O Great Prince, permit us to express the sorrow which fills our hearts, as Christians and as men, in contemplating the probability of war in any portion of the continent of Europe. Deeply to be deplored would it be, were that peace, which to a very large extent has happily prevailed so many years, exchanged for the unspeakable horrors of war, with all it's attendant moral evil and physical suffering.

It is not our business, nor do we presume to offer any opinion upon the question now at issue between the Imperial Government of Russia and that of any other country; but, estimating the exalted position in which Divine Providence has placed thee, and the solemn responsibilities devolving upon thee, not only as an earthly potentate, but also as a believer in that Gospel which proclaims 'Peace on earth', and 'Goodwill toward men', we implore Him by whom 'kings reign and princes decree justice' so to

Deputation to the Czar

influence thy heart and to direct thy councils at this momentous crisis that thou mayst practically exhibit to the nations, and even to those who profess the 'like precious faith', the efficacy of the Gospel of Christ, and the universal application of His command, 'Love your enemies; bless them that curse you; do good to them that hate you; and pray for them that despitefully use you and persecute you; that ye may be the children of your Father which is in Heaven'.

The more fully the Christian is persuaded of the justice of his own cause, the greater his magnanimity in the exercise of forbearance. May the Lord make thee the honoured instrument of exemplifying this true nobility; thereby securing to thyself and to thy vast dominions that true glory and those rich blessings, which could never result from the most successful appeal to arms.

Thus, O mighty Prince, may the miseries and devastation of war be averted; and in the solemn day when 'every one of us shall give account of himself to God', may the benediction of the Redeemer apply to thee, 'Blessed are the peacemakers, for they shall be called the children of God'; and mayst thou be permitted, through a Saviour's love, to exchange an earthly for a heavenly crown, 'a crown of glory which fadeth not away'.

The Friend published the text of the Address and the Emperor's reply in March 1854. *The Times* and some other newspapers published the Address and the full Russian reply, signed by Count Nesselrode, both in French, as it was given to the delegation, and the English translation.

The Emperor, after listening with kind attention to the Address, said he wished to offer some explanation of his views as to the cause of the present unhappy differences:

We received the blessings of Christianity from the Greek Empire, and this has established and maintained ever since a link of connection, both moral and religious, between Russia and that power. The ties that have thus united the two countries have existed for nine hundred years, and were not severed by the conquest of Russia by the Tartars. When at a later period our country succeeded in shaking off that yoke, and the Greek Empire in its turn fell under the sway of the Turks, we still continued to take a lively interest in the welfare of our co-religionists there. When Russia became powerful enough to resist the Turks, and to dictate the terms of peace, we paid particular attention to the well-being of the Greek Church, and procured the insertion in successive treaties, of most important articles in her favour. I myself have acted as my predecessors had done, and the Treaty of Adrianople in 1829 was as explicit as the former ones in this respect. Turkey on her part, recognised this right of religious interference, and fulfilled her engagements until the last year or two, when for the first time, she gave me reason to complain. I will not now avert to the parties who were her principal instigators on that occasion, suffice it to say, that it became my duty to interfere, and to claim from Turkey the fulfilment of her engagements. My representations were pressing but friendly, and I have every reason to believe that the matters would soon have been settled, if Turkey had not been induced by other parties to believe that I had ulterior objects in view; and that I was aiming at conquest, aggrandizement and the ruin of Turkey. I have solemnly disclaimed, and do now as solemnly disclaim, every such motive. I do not desire war, I abhor it as sincerely as you do, and am ready to forget the past, if only the opportunity be afforded me.

I have great esteem for your country, and a sincere affection for your Queen, whom I admire not only as a Sovereign, but as a lady, a wife, and a mother. I have placed full confidence in her and have acted towards her in a frank and friendly spirit. I felt it my duty to draw her attention to future dangers, which I considered as likely sooner or later to arise in the East, in consequence of the existing state of things. What on my part was prudent foresight, has been unfairly construed in your country into a designing policy, and an ambitious desire of conquest. This has deeply wounded my feelings and afflicted my heart. Personal insults and invective I regard with indifference. It is beneath my dignity to notice them. I am ready to forgive all that is personal to me, and to hold out my hand to my enemies in the true Christian spirit. I cannot understand what cause of complaint your nation has against Russia. I am anxious to avoid war by all possible means, I will not attack, and shall only act in self defence; but I cannot be indifferent to what concerns the honour of my country. I have a duty to perform as a Sovereign. As a Christian I am ready to comply with the precepts of religion. On the present occasion, my great duty is to attend to the interests and honour of my country.

The deputation then remarked that, as their mission was not of a political character, but intended to convey to the Emperor the sentiments of their own Society as a religious body, they did not feel it their place to enter into any of the questions involved in the present dispute; but with the Emperor's permission, they would be glad to call his attention to a few points. These points are explained in Robert Charleton's letters written soon after the interview.

Letter from Robert Charleton to his wife, Catherine

We yesterday saw the Emperor, who not only allowed us to read the Address, but gave us time to make such additional remarks as we thought desirable. Baron Nicolay acted as interpreter the Emperor speaking in French. We have made notes of the Emperor's Address to us and shall bring with us a statement of what passed at the interview with, I hope, considerable accuracy.

The tone of the Emperor's remarks was conciliatory and agreeable. The outline of what the deputation stated, J. Sturge being the speaker, after reading the Address and explaining the constitution of the Meeting for Sufferings from whom it emanated, was that neither the Society of Friends, nor a large proportion of the rightly thinking part of the English public, approved of the inflammatory tone of the press in England, in relation to the question in dispute. That many of us had incurred unpopularity with those who wished to depend on physical force, by advocating the settlement of international disputes by arbitration. That, whereas the followers of Mahomet avowedly justified an appeal to arms as a means of spreading their faith, the reign of Him, on whom the Christian rested his hopes of salvation, was to be, emphatically, one of Peace; and that in case of a European war, amongst the multitude who would be the victims, those who were the principal cause of the war would probably not suffer the most, but innocent men with their wives and children.

On our thanking the Emperor for the manner in which he had received us, and saying that it would be gratefully appreciated by those who had deputed us to present the Address, and that though we should probably never see him again on this side of Eternity, we wished him to know there were those in England who as sincerely desired his temporal and spiritual welfare as his own subjects. He shook hands with us all very cordially, and with eyes moistened with emotion, turned hastily away, as we believe to conceal his feelings, saying 'my wife also wishes to see you'. We were accordingly introduced into the Empress's apartment, where we spent ten minutes in conversation with her and her daughter, the Duchess Olga, both of whom were able to speak English pretty well.

This morning we have been making calls on Sir Hamilton Seymour, The British Ambassador; also on the British Consul Baron Steigliz, and others, to whom we had letters of introduction, but whom we thought it best not to see until after we had accomplished our mission.

67

On the whole we have proceeded with as little difficulty, and as much satisfaction to ourselves, and I hope to those by whom we were deputed, as could have been reasonably expected; and it presents matter for thankfulness that so little impediment has arisen.

The next letter written by Robert Charleton to his uncle repeats some of the information contained in his letter to his wife. The letter to his uncle is taken from the original while the letter written on the 11th and 12th is from Catherine Charleton's note book as the original has not survived. Both letters show the sense of relief that they have presented the Address to the Emperor, after what must have seemed a long and anxious wait. Clearly they realised that they must not accept a gift from the Emperor which could be interpreted as a bribe. The English press would have made the most out of even the smallest souvenir.

There seems to have been some difference of opinion as to the name of the Grand Duchess they saw with the Empress; it was probably the Grand Duchess Olga.

This letter, although regretting the delay in their departure from St. Petersburg, points out the need for a meeting to be arranged with Meeting for Sufferings as soon as they return to London. His estimated time of arrival in London is surprisingly accurate considering the difficulties of the journey and the increasingly cold weather. In fact they improved on the estimate and arrived on 5th day evening.

Letter from Robert Charleton to his Uncle, Samuel Fox

PETERSBURG 2 MO 13 1854

My dear Uncle,

I presume thou wilt have seen Joseph Sturge's letter to Joseph Cooper giving an account of our interview with the Emperor, including an outline of the remarks that were made by the deputation. Although both the Address itself, and our own note to Count Nesselrode written the day after our arrival, distinctly disclaim for our mission anything of a political character, yet the Emperor thought fit to take the opportunity of giving us an account of the causes which had led to the present unhappy embroilment. We shall bring with us a carefully prepared statement of what the Emperor said; and I will only now remark that there was an earnest straight forward manner in all he said, which tended very much to confirm the opinion repeatedly and strongly expressed to us by W. C. Gellibrand and A. Mirrilies, the parties particularly named by John Venning, that the Emperor, however mistaken he may be on some points, has acted in this business from a sense of principle. It must be extremely difficult for a man in his situation to obtain the means of forming a strictly impartial judgement on the matters involved in this dispute. I believe that the apparent want of candour in some of the proceedings of the Russian Government may be explained without impugning the Emperor's sincerity.

We had fixed to leave this morning on our journey homewards, but Baron Nicolay called on us yesterday, to say that if we could postpone our departure until tomorrow afternoon, the Emperor would like for us to be the bearers of a written reply to the Address we have presented; and that, in that case the Grand Duchess Marie of Leuchtenberg, and probably too their heir apparent, and other members of the Imperial family, would like to see us at 12 o'clock tomorrow. To this proposal we of course assented; the Baron stating that in order that this delay might not materially retard our journey, they were willing to send on a Government Courier, to arrange that there should be no delay in procuring horses, between this and the Russian frontier, much detention being often experienced from this cause.

I feel quite concerned to see the government attach so much importance to our visit here, appearing to expect from it results which we fear there is little prospect of being realised. But although we have again and again disclaimed anything political in connexion with our present mission; yet if the government here, in the present suspended state of diplomatic relations, wish to avail themselves of the opportunity of our return to England for making any representations at home, which may tend to subserve the main object of our mission. I think it would be our duty not to shrink from any responsibility which might thus be imposed on us; due caution being, of course, exercised not in any way to compromise either ourselves or the religious society to which we belong.

Since we have been in Russia we have not seen the slightest appearance of popular enthusiasm in favour of war; but the longer we remain here, the more distinctly we see that, among the more intelligent and influential classes there exists, together with an earnest desire for peace, a profound sympathy with the Emperor, in the full persuasion that he is acting conscientiously, and for the real good of his country.

Baron Nicolay when he was with us yesterday said that it was the Emperor's wish to make us some little present, by way of a souvenir of Petersburg, but not knowing exactly how to do this in the way most

69

agreeable to our feelings he asked us to mention if there was any one thing that we should prefer to another, to guide the Emperor in his choice. We do not doubt that this offer was made with perfect sincerity and good feeling, but we have thought it best to write a note to Baron Nicolay this morning, to the effect, that whilst gratefully appreciating the Emperor's kindness and condescension, we thought that under the circumstances of our present mission it would be best for us respectfully to decline it, explaining, that our single and earnest desire being to contribute any influence we might possess or acquire in promoting the cause of international peace; we feared that the moral effect of any representation we might make in our own country might be weakened in some quarters, if it were known that we had accepted such a present.

Under the idea that we should leave Petersburg today, we called on seventh day on Sir Hamilton Seymour the British Ambassador. He entirely concurs in the wisdom of the course we adopted in communicating with Count Nesselrode direct and not through him. He is about leaving Petersburg for England, although not immediately from the present state of things, which under the present circumstances we cannot but regret. Notwithstanding our delay in starting from Petersburg, I still hope we may arrive in London on 6th day evening, but we shall probably write again from Berlin, or send a telegraphic message from a further point if that should be needful. It seems very desirable that we should see some of the members of the Meeting for Sufferings with the least possible delay after our arrival, to consult what is best to be done as to waiting on our own government. Whilst it seems almost burdensome to see so much importance attached to our visit, yet I cannot but regard the very eagerness with which the government seem to seize hold of so feeble an instrumentality, as an additional proof of the Emperor's sincere desire for peace, and of his anxious wish to avert the calamity of war, in any manner which may be consistent with what he honestly considers to be the true honour and interest of his country.

The weather has become much colder than when we entered Russia, the thermometer during the last few days having ranged between 6 and 12 degrees Fahrenheit, but this morning I noticed it down to -3 i.e. 3 degrees below zero or 35 degrees below freezing, and in exposed situations I find it has been down to -7, or 39 degrees below freezing. We have not experienced any inconvenience from it, and are favoured to enjoy good health. With love from my companions and self, to thyself and our dear friends to whom we are so indebted for their kind interest and solicitude on our behalf.

I am thy affectionate nephew,

Robert Charleton

Letter from Henry Pease to his son, Henry Fell

ST. PETERSBURG 6TH DAY

My dear Boy,

Had ample time been mine I proposed to have written to thy Uncle Fry but cannot send him a suitable letter. But I must tell thee with what deep concern I hear of the death of thy Uncle I. H. Fell, but at this distance what can I say, or do?

Just returned from the Emperor with whom we sat and had the reception, shake of the hand, thrice, repeated. In parting, 'My wife wants to see you'. So we were with the Empress and Grand Duchess Mary about fifteen minutes. I write to save post and cannot give particulars.

Thou might send a letter to be at Hughe's by 5th day week.

Let thy Uncle Fry know of this.

With my best love

Thy very affectionate father,

Henry Pease

71

CHAPTER VII

Delayed Departure

HENRY PEASE'S LETTERS to his nephews were probably intended to be passed around the family. 'My dear Nephew E.P.Jr.' would be Edward Pease Jr. eldest son of Joseph Pease. This letter clearly shows how anxious Henry was to leave Russia as soon as the Address had been presented, and to get safely home. It is one of the few letters which contain any criticism of his travelling companions when he writes:'My much respected companions have more caution and perhaps less push than I have or I guess I should have seen home days earlier than their movements admit of'. Although he was not the youngest, he was forty seven, and Robert Charleton was forty five, he seems to have been the fittest and most active. He did not like the delay to see the Grand Duchess of Leuchtenberg, and thought that it was some devious diplomatic plot to keep them in Russia. In his next letter written to his son, he just comments that it was not worth the delay.

It seems to have been Henry Richard in his biography, *Memoirs of Joseph Sturge*, who paraphrases Charleton's letter and makes, quite possibly as a result of a later conversation with Sturge, a conjecture into a certainty:

We called [says Charleton] at the Palace of the Grand Duchess as proposed. But here our reception was very different from what it had been a few days before at the Imperial Palace. Instead of the earnest and cordial manner of the Emperor and Empress, the Grand Duchess received us with merely formal politeness. Her sorrowful air and the depressed look of the gentleman in waiting, made it evident that a great change had come over the whole aspect of affairs. Nor were we at a loss to account for the change. The mail from England had arrived, with newspapers giving an account of the opening of Parliament and of the intensely warlike speeches in the House of Commons.

This conjectural interpretation of the events of 14th February has been accepted and echoed by all of those who have since written about the incident at the Duchess's Palace; but Stephen Frick thought it worthwhile to investigate whether or not what the deputation thought was happening was in fact what actually happened. His conclusion was that they were right in assuming that something was troubling the Russians, but they were understandingly mistaken as to cause of the anxiety.

Dispatches in the Public Record Office show that a courier could make the winter trip between London and St. Petersburg, depending on the weather, in somewhere between seven and ten days. In 1854 Parliament opened on 31st January, and had the Emperor wanted news of the speeches there, he could have had them in hand at least a day or two before he met the deputation on 10th February. If he had been disposed to he could have shown his displeasure at that meeting, instead of receiving the deputation so warmly. But the Emperor and his court were not waiting for news of Parliament. They were much more concerned with Clarendon's reply to the demand for 'juste reciprocite', a hard diplomatic fact that would leave no more room for compromise, should it not be an answer to Brunnow's liking. That reply and Brunnow's subsequent action reached St. Petersburg on Monday, 13th February. On that day, at twenty minutes before two o'clock, Hamilton Seymour was informed by Nesselrode that diplomatic relations between England and Russia had been suspended. The deputation would know nothing of this, but by noon on Tuesday the Emperor's daughter would. The Friends were fortunate that their reception was at least polite, for it must have been this news that caused the chilly reaction of the Duchess of Leuchtenberg.

The Friends were lucky that after this dramatic change in the situation, the Emperor still kept his word and sent a courier to help them on their return journey. In spite of Henry Pease's fears there were no other delays so that the deputation left St. Petersburg on Tuesday afternoon.

Letter from Henry Pease to his nephew – possibly the brother of Elizabeth Pease Gibson

ST. PETERSBURG 1ST DAY

My dear Nephew,

Whilst I wonder sometimes almost to a doubt of the fact, at the unmerited kindness of my relatives, I luxuriate in the affections I bear them and in this feeling I offer thee one of my 'sorry' notes. I wrote to dear E.P.G. from Konigsberg, and have written home twice since, so that from thence you may be in possession of items repeated in this, which I cannot avoid.

Parting from Konigsberg we patiently worked off six miles per hour the six hundred and fifty miles to this place in a week including three nights and less first day at Riga, thou canst believe it was very acceptable to enter upon apartments both comfortable and well adapted to our wants, and after three days dinners in the carriage (odds) to drop in here for a two dinner system (i.e. lunch and dinner) is a consideration, in short when thou visits this city, quarter at Miss Benson's English Quay.

From Riga our carriage has been on a sledge and sometimes we have swept over the ground in good style. Once at midnight our carriage was laid over as far as the sledge would allow it to go, it was a cold tedious affair but we were none the worse. At seven the same morning after most extraordinary thundering over snow drifts, we thundered against one and came to a stand, happily not far from a station. We travelled with various numbers of horses, our Courier having to compromise when they wanted us to take more than we required, we never exceeded seven i.e. four at the wheel and three before, these the yamshick drives rope in hand, the charge in Russia is about one and a half-pence per mile per horse, they are small but active and of good courage.

The post house masters are limited by laws, they have the stations and stables rent free with as much wood as they require to burn. These stations are fourteen to eighteen miles apart and are really for the most part very respectable erections with ground floor only, having well finished and furnished rooms, for the day, two bedrooms, with very large fold yards for general purposes besides the post horses, and these are numerous. At one place we had a little delay, sixty horse being out; these houses are built so much to a plan that being sleepy one might suppose merely a return to that you had left. But alluding to horses I must tell thee of my admiration of the horses in this city, they are not very large but such well bred compact animals dashing along at twelve to fifteen miles per hour in the handsomely appointed sledges, one or two, when the latter one is in the shafts and the other on the side in traces, with a rein to pull his head to one side down to his knee, this I suppose to imitate the antique, and no journey here has, of course, had first place, and we have not done much in sightseeing.

On 7th day we sent a note to Count Nesselrode, requesting he would name a time when we might call to explain to him the nature of our mission. In a few hours he sent a messenger, I think one of his upper officials, with a civil note appointing one o-clock today, second day, and the messenger was instructed to offer to accompany us to any objects of interest.

74

This morning we received a message from the Count stating that the Emperor having sent for him he would not be at liberty until 1-30, this no doubt was done to prevent our having to wait for him, a piece of consideration officials don't show. Of course we were there at 1-30 and had but a short wait in a large room fitted up in an effective but plain style, it was a pleasure to study. Count N. received us with true courteous politeness, and had us all seated viz. a viz. listened to the Address, expressed satisfaction and said that the Emperor would appoint a time to express his hearty concurrence in the sentiments it contained. We requested to know whether it was probable we should have the pleasure of seeing the heir apparent, and of reading as well as presenting the Address to which he answered in the affirmative. We thanked him for his attention and retired, he coming out of the room and renewing the offer of an escort to places of interest. We now wait a summons to the Emperor, which accomplished, all our feelings are homeward without much delay though we purpose to see chiefly what is to be seen here.

Since we were well housed here the weather has become much colder, this morning 6 degrees above zero with a steady breeze, minute particles of ice glistening in the brilliant sunshine with a pure blue sky. Thou must imagine under such circumstances the trees laden with coral on a grand scale, thou must imagine their beauty for I can by no means convey the ten thousandth part of a worthy idea of it.

We had a long walk to the dead market, frozen things of all kinds on stalls and in sledge loads, fish being divided into slices by the persevering use of the mallet and huge knife, pigs on their hind legs in mockery of attitude of prayer, partridges in abundance hares 1s 10d each, plenty of blackcock 3s 6d per brace and so on. We also went to see the stores of live fish on the Neva, i.e. stocks kept of those caught in the Autumn and placed on a vessel through which the water runs.

This afternoon we had a sledge drive down the Neva to the open gulf, one broad expanse of ice, the track is indicated by posts at short distances and every three miles there is a watch van in which three men live, this van has a bell which is constantly used in fog or snow storm, this road being very dangerous at such a time.

Whatever the cold outside we are most comfortable in our rooms here, without being close they are a most genial temperature throughout, so agreeable to reconcile the absence, for a time, of an open fire of Adelaides, each room has two stoves constantly throwing out a gentle warmth which double windows and very thick walls contribute to retain, so that muslin curtains and plants thriving in the windows, however little compatible with our English notions of winter, have a light cheerful appearance.

We have received several civilities here, Mr. Gellibrand, an eminent merchant and friend of the Wheelers, engages us to dine there tomorrow, he has also entered our names at the Public Library. Another merchant, Mr. Mirrilies invited us to dine on the fourth day, we did not fix, another family connected with the Imperial household invited us to call, declined; the British Consul called; and afterwards sent a card of admission to the Hermitage. I apprehend we could have constant visiting if we wished it.

We came here to represent Christian's precept as opposed to war but the commercial one is no trifle, in this respect Russia is comparatively a young country and a very large portion of the capital so employed in this city is English, in connection with flax, corn, tallow, etc. which are obtained from the interior on the advance to the traders by the merchants here of three-quarters or upwards of the whole value intended to be brought down six or eight days hence, one merchant said their house advanced 2 to 300,000 pounds yearly that way and it answered their purpose, this year merchants dare not do it and the Winter fairs inland have been very much affected, besides the English houses are becoming uneasy and either withdrawing capital or transferring it to Russians. Tea, sugar and other things are becoming dearer.

Sixth day. Day after day passed without our summons to the Palace, it came last evening for 1.30 to-day. We have occupied some of our time in visits to objects of interest specially the Hermitage, a palace of prodigious grandeur devoted to works of Art, how often have I thought of my friend Gibson and thee in going through those continuous rooms of paintings including many from the old masters. The Mining Corps, a great collection of splendid minerals and most complete model of machinery, and the Ice Hills occupied part of yesterday.

2-30 we had half-an-hour with the Emperor and three shakes of the hand, we can not speak of results, his behaviour was all we could wish, – 'My wife wants to see you'. We were about fifteen minutes with the Empress and Grand Duchess Mary.

I cannot give details this is written hastily to save post.

With every dear love to each assure thy friends.

Thy very closely attached Uncle,

Henry

76

Letter from Henry Pease to his nephew, Edward Pease Jr.

ST. PETERSBURG 7TH DAY 11/2/54

My dear Nephew, E.P.Jr.

As I hesitate to inflict too much of my correspondence upon any of my dear relatives, it is very pleasant to feel that there are yet several that have had no reason to complain, and remembering thy capable shoulders, I propose then to throw on them sheets of however similar materials of very dissimilar size and contents to those the burden of which thou hast in part to bear. Having yesterday posted a letter to thy dear Grandpa stating the very 'gracious' and patient hearing we had with the Aristocrat of all the Russias. I shall probably not post this until Konigsberg, where all well, we expect to spend tomorrow week to my notion we might just as well have been quite as far as Berlin. My respected companions have more caution and perhaps less push than I have or, I guess, I should have seen home some days earlier than their movements admit of; but there is comfort in finding one can submit to others even where it is a positive cross to ones own decided longing, as is the case in point, and it is not improbable that even when as I hope the really tedious journey from this to Konigsberg is accomplished and even the civilised modes of travelling to London may have safely returned us there, we may find some matters connected with this mission that will call for the use of strong bands to restrain my longing, in the mean time the idea of beginning in a few hours to notch off the 'Versts' is the pleasant subject to reflect upon.

There can be no surprise that trade is dull, trade tends to the comfort and civilisation, war to misery and degradation, so that if half the world is taxing its best energies to provide misery there can be no reasonable chance of trade.

In a few words I noted in my last the accomplishment of the culminating point of our mission from different sources we shall obtain a very correct report of what passed with the Emperor, and as we have no right to look for any special result, it is perhaps safer for us to agree on what was stated, and bring with us rather than trusting to individual memory to write to our friends, the 'Emperor said' so. We have distinct permission to make what use we like of what transpired; of one thing there is no doubt, that whether caused by the union and stern aspect of E. and F. or the neutrality or enmity of other powers, or any other causes the Emperor would gladly avoid war, in his position many reasons for this must press upon him. A very few of which petty Mortals can see, Russia, though of vast extent, and

77

unmeasurable resources if opened out on free trade principles, is comparatively young, the life blood of the government revenues is to a large extent caused by British capital and the trade with England is nine-tenths of the exports at Cronstadt. The system is for the merchants to pay down a large portion of the value of the goods to be delivered on 9th or 10th month, to pay this down say in 1st or 2nd months, this year they dare not do it. The government officers demand the tax the peasants reply, here is our tallow and our hemp, take it, 'no we will have money' and now I learn vigorous means are being used to obtain it.

So much as to money; now as to men; a new conscription note is just issued in nearly all the provinces requiring 10 in 1000, in a few provinces 9 or 8, and three provinces near the seat of the war, where the people are already oppressed by the presence of the troops, are excused, this conscription will raise 300,000 men being the second in 8 months. I believe an awful liberal supply of 'Cannon food' for one country to provide in addition to the 800,000 regulars and about 600,000 liable to garrison duty. Now thou art aware that in Russia there is no middle class, what then? Why the men are serfs, the property of noble men, and every serf pays his master so much per annum varying in degree to his position, as it is the case in this house the serf, our waiter, has a city situation he probably, as near as I recollect, pays his owner 35 roubles a year say £6, another on the estate village may pay £4, now if a man has a great number of these the conscription makes an income small by degrees and disagreeably less, at least the nobles it is said think so, enough on that point.

But in the midst of this, instigated it is said by the Emperor, is a gradually swelling religious enthusiasm, which has now risen so high that its reflex if peace were declared might be attended with unpleasant consequences, for what is a multitude of blind enthusiastic servant girls to think of their adored Emperor, if at one time he urges them on to fight for the cross and sends a commission to ascertain particulars as to the appearance of an angel seen during a battle causing the Turks to draw back, and at another calls them back without reason.

So much for the internal view of things, then look at the complexity of the external, and if thou canst point out an easy way for the Emperor to extricate himself from his difficulties, thou mayst rely upon his favour.

Thou will rightly think this very dry, I will then turn back to 6th day; I am going to Count Nesselrode's office, and being shown into a lower office a door opposite where we sat had been left slightly open through this one ought to see another window but ever and anon a new head interposed having staring eyes, which in turn gave place to a similar formation of the human species. Shortly in comes a slight but well made official in gorgeous uniform, Baron Nicholas, and in a most pleasant simple manner said, 'I shall have the pleasure of going with you to his Majesty': a short drive brought us to the Palace, plenty of fellows to open the carriage door, to take our cloaks, and plenty of guards in the hall. A very likely looking palace servant dressed in black with scarlet stripes here and there, and a beautiful black plume in his cap leads the way upstairs, where one or two parties had taken convenient stand to obtain a sight of the strangers.

Upstairs, upstairs, along galleries, through rooms, here soldiers of one province, there attendants of another sort, arrived at top, there stood three fine fellows in white uniform, bright helmets and spears who had there to bide their turn allowed to evince as much animation as the stones they stood upon; enter the anti-room a little before time, chat with Baron N. at the window looking down upon the Neva, talk about sledge races, and the burning of the Palace a few years since, try to appear at ease when in reality it was not just so, observe he who keeps the door of the Emperor's cabinet has no armour or sword, he is nearly black, quite eastern in costume with a scarlet turban.

Enter the Emperor, coldly inclines towards us, a fine powerful tall frame with an unmistakable countenance which one thinks quite capable of saying 'Siberia' although by no means incapable of genuine kindly relaxation. The double doors being fairly shut he ventured to shake hands with us, respecting the interview, I have not much to add at present, the details had better be correctly given, I think I stated to thy dear Grandpa that at parting the Emperor not only shook our hands as we rose from our seats but accompanied us to the door and most heartily shook our hands again.

Although it had been our wish faithfully to discharge our mission, and on careful retrospection I do not see that more could be done. Having said, 'My wife wants to see you', we were again escorted I can't tell thee where, but listless well fed, liveried, and wondering attendants abounded everywhere a part of the 5,000 constant residents of the Imperial Palace, until the large folding gilt doors were opened for us to enter the Empress's suite of rooms. She though ladylike is very shaky, and has been so since the desperate deeds on the Emperor's ascending the throne, her salutation was, 'I have seen the Emperor with tears in his eyes'. We were then requested to sit down and remained a short quarter of an hour with her and the Grand

Duchess Olga, not Mary as I stated in my last, the latter speaking to me seemed to think that it was not just, that the English should fraternise with an Emperor of a year and deal so hardly with one who had been 30 years or nearly before the world. Not liking to stare about the room I cannot give thee much idea beyond that with furniture and flowers and large camelias in bloom, carving and gilding, it was just as grand as a man could design it ; so much that I may have wearied thee but yet my story must go on. I have written a large part of the foregoing on 1st day every time my companions retired to rest and now past 11, I am dowdy enough.

On 7th day we got our passports, got our carriage brought out, paid accounts, and as per the commencement of this talked about leaving at 8 am. on 2nd day if nothing prevented but with a lurking doubt whether it would be so.

This first day afternoon we had a procession of callers among them Baron Hegltz the Emperor's banker, and said to be in his confidence, on coming in he said 'I am glad I found you in'. He remained nearly an hour and we had an open discussion of affairs connected with our mission, the case was put in various ways, each offering a notion more or less appropriate how peace might be sought, he enquired when we were going, why we hurried and so forth, and after rising from his seat stood as if 'absorbed', and most pleasantly took his leave. He is a deep eyed, black headed, sagacious looking man in the prime of life, said to be a good man as a man.

J.S. and I went over the Neva to take leave of C. Gellibrand and wife who have been kind friends , and strongly pressed our tarriance. 'Many want to see you'. 'Good seed is being sown'. We were out about an hour, on our return Baron Nicholas had just called ; 'Count Nesselrode wishes me to say three things.

1st. the Emperor wishes you to remain until Tuesday, that he may prepare an answer to the Address, it will be what his Majesty said to you, but it will be in two languages and signed by Count N. so that it will be authentic.

2nd. the Grand Duchess of Leuchtenburgh who was in England in the summer wishes you to call at 12.30 on Tuesday.

3rd. in order to make up to you this delay the Count will send before you a Government Courier to prepare horses and take all the trouble by which he thinks you will not lose more than two hours in reaching Konigsberg, and there is yet another matter the Emperor is desirous you should take with you a souvenir in remembrance of your visit to the Palace, and he requests you to inform him what you would select that it may be acceptable to you'.

We reply that if it is the Emperor's wish, we will remain and will call upon the Duchess L. as appointed. As we are desirous to return home without delay we shall probably accept Count N's offer as to the Courier, and in respect of the Emperor's very kind offer we will send up a note tomorrow. We were unanimous that we ought to have no gifts, but did ever the Emperor hear of such a thing as a refusal? And how is it to be done?

We have had a tug of it, to put our note right, so as to admit of no incorrect interpretation and have about satisfied ourselves subject to tomorrows revision. But how will it be taken? Indeed daily we are in positions requiring careful thought and some anxiety. Even now we have our doubts, may they prove groundless, whether we shall be allowed to leave on 3rd day, that is the day Count Orloff is expected. It is said that he has entirely failed in his mission to Austria, and if not for this, Count Orloff, why detain us till that day. We already have before us what we know has Count N's sanction, and no doubt the Emperor's, as to what he said to us, and who believes that Duchess L. could not have asked for the call for tomorrow, and would not have asked for it at all but for some court purposes. I am not at all in the humour to complain, except if this is bad purpose, if we can by any personal sacrifice serve the cause which has brought us here, but we must not be drawn into a Labyrinth of Diplomacy. It is now past noon of night and time to give up.

2nd day. On my morning look at the thermometer I found it three degrees below zero, it has been six nearer the river. This helps a little to reconcile to not travelling, indeed J.S. has a slight rheumatic affection and R.C. has been a little off food, so they appear very comfortable indoors. Our friend Gellibrand has called. We have suggested that the English here should write a letter expressive of their estimate of the Emperor's character, the kind consideration shown them, the harm done by newspaper attacks, etc. this will be done I expect.

Dorpat 5th day evening. I could have posted this at Petersburg, but thought that part of the way we should gain on the post, not so, there is too much snow, our progress is very slow.

Riga 7th day 15th 11 a.m. Just arrived. Since 6 a.m. yesterday constant tug through snow which has sadly delayed us. We may be in London 6th day night. Please send letters to be there that day 7th. All well, I will write from thence. Home is my desire at the earliest suitable chance. We have snowy winds today and are 250 miles from Konigsberg so plans are uncertain. I have letters from H.F.P. and Sister Gibson. I feel it a great loss to be so long out of the society of my dear relatives; but I am spared uneasiness respecting them to a degree that induces the hopes, that my coming here has not been wrong.

This second day morning post has brought me a letter from my dear H.F.P. I feel much the kindness of his relatives in writing to him. My love is ever to the family band and many more to W.E.P.; W. Mansor; W. Jones; J. F. Clapham; A. Thorpe. If thou approve of this attempt to interest thee would it be too much trouble to send a short summary of it to J. T. Hardwin with my love.

Henry Pease

Henry Pease

CHAPTER VIII

The Return Journey

IT WAS WITH A GREAT SENSE of relief that the travellers left St. Petersburg and started for home. They must have been worried in case the Emperor thought of some other reason to delay their departure, especially after the cold reception they had had from the Grand Duchess of Leuchtenberg. The changeable weather also caused some anxiety, as a general thaw would have made travelling impossible. If the ice on the rivers had started to melt it would have been too dangerous to drive across, and there would have been considerable delay before the possibility of crossing by boat. It was for this reason that they reluctantly agreed to travel on Sunday.

They left St. Petersburg on Tuesday, 14th February, in the afternoon, and they reached London in the evening of Thursday, 23rd February. The journey to St. Petersburg took thirteen days, the return journey only nine days; almost as fast as a Government Courier who could make the winter trip between London and St. Petersburg in somewhere between seven and ten days, depending on the weather.

It was on the return trip that their worst accident occurred. Henry Pease describes it as 'a real roll over', while Robert Charleton says that he and his companions were 'altogether in a heap'. This descriptive phrase Catherine Charleton put brackets round in her note book, no doubt considering it as too undignified, to be printed.

Letter from Robert Charleton to his wife, Catherine

DORPAT 2 MONTH 16TH FIFTH-DAY EVENING

When we left Petersburg on Third-day afternoon the road was in capital order, and we proceeded a few stages, our carriage on the sledge, with considerable rapidity; but in the course of the night there came on a snow storm, with a high wind, which by the morning had caused great drifts in the road, that greatly obstructed our progress. In attempting to pass one enormous drift near Narva, which nearly blocked our road, our carriage was entirely upset, and the head of the carriage being somewhat lower down the bank than the wheels we were altogether in a heap, but coming down on soft snow, we were

83

not at all hurt, which is cause for much thankfulness. By the help of a number of peasants, who soon came to our assistance, we got the carriage upright in half-an-hour, and proceeded on our journey, the carriage not being materially damaged.

Through-out the day, however, we proceeded very heavily on account of the quantity of snow, and we were once or twice stuck fast in a drift, from which it required a number of men to extricate us. We had intended to proceed through the night, but as the existing state of things would have made that both difficult and unsafe, we lodged in a country post house, at a place called Raima Paagern, where we found tolerable accommodation.

During most of yesterday it rather thawed, the thermometer having risen forty degrees during two days, from 5° below zero to 35°, and during last night there was a further considerable fall of snow; so that we began to fear that we should be quite stopped. Happily, however, the last fall of snow was not accompanied by wind; so that when we started this morning, although the snow was very deep, it had not drifted, and we were therefore able to proceed at a slow pace; but although we had been travelling a night and two days, we are only two hundred and twenty miles on our way from Petersburg. Today the weather is fine with a return of frost; but the snow is not sufficiently beaten to make it prudent to travel by night; we therefore lodge here tonight, and start tomorrow morning for Riga, which we hope to reach on Seventh-day morning. It is 180 miles from hence.

Before leaving Petersburg on Third-day we waited on the Duchess of Leuchtenberg, agreeably with her request, and were admitted to a short interview, during which nothing particular passed on either side. We could not, however, avoid the painful conclusion, from many incidental circumstances, that during the last few days the probability is lessened of a pacific solution of the present unhappy dispute. We suppose that the arrival of the news from England, with the tone of the debates in Parliament, leave very small reason for hoping that the English and French Governments will consent to any terms which the Emperor would consider consistent with his dignity and the honour of his country; so that, as far as human sight can go, the alternative of war seems almost inevitable. This is truly affecting; but we know that even the most untoward events are under the control of a superintending Power, and are made subservient to the accomplishment of His designs. Under any circumstances we cannot but feel satisfaction in having made an attempt, however feeble, to contribute something towards averting the dreaded result.

Very great kindness has been shown us by the English residents at Petersburg. On the evening before we left we met a large party at W. C. Gellibrand's, including Dr. Law, the English Church clergyman T. S. Ellerby, minister of the English and American Independent Church; Dr. Handyside, an eminent Scottish physician settled here, and a number of leading merchants, etc. and also of ladies. We thought it best to read the Address to them. They expressed a warm approval of the document, and much interest in our visit, and its object. It will be impossible for us to do otherwise than retain a grateful sense of the kindness we have received from these truly estimable persons, and, indeed, from all classes. For, on the day before our departure, we had a very friendly call from an old Russian Admiral, who is much respected; and on the afternoon of our leaving, we also had a long call from Baron Nicolay, an attache of Count Nesselrode's, from whom we have experienced much and persevering kindness. We had also farewell calls before leaving from Dr. Law, W. C. Gellibrand, Dr. Handyside, T. S. Ellerby, A. Mirrilies, Charles Nottbeck, etc, so that our time was pretty fully taken up.

During most of the time since we left Petersburg the weather has been cloudy, but for some hours before sunset this afternoon we had a fine clear sky with bright sunshine, which was quite a treat. The effect of the rays falling obliquely through the pine forests, with the boughs laden with snow, was exquisite. It reminded me of the lines: 'In the solemn depths of the forest shade'. As we expect to travel from Konigsberg almost as fast as the mail, I expect that this will not reach thee many days before our return. In the hope of being permitted through Divine favour to meet very shortly.

I am thy truly affectionate husband,

Robert Charleton

Letter from Henry Pease to his son, Henry Fell Pease

DORPAT 5TH DAY 16/2/54

My dear Boy,

I cannot quite make out what letters thou hast received from me, but I have written pretty often, and on Second-day I was glad of one from thee. There does not seem much good in my again referring to the affecting death of thy uncle J. H. Fell, mine on the subject would cross thine on the road. I knew thou wouldst feel it although you have

85

not been much together lately, you were likely to be so in future life. My last to thee just missed our having presented the Address to the Emperor, it was well done at the time, as we quite thought we saw a change towards the English within a few days after and that had we been later the Emperor might not have shown us so much attention.

On the Seventh-day we had several calls to make, in the afternoon, I went to see a celebrated church, the granite columns are surprising, there must be fifty of them rising forty feet high three feet six inches in diameter, each column one piece, the altar nearly all massive silver, but there was so much bowing to the ground muttering prayers and making the sign of the cross before particular Saints that I came away thoroughly depressed because I feared the form was taken for the substance. Then to see Peter the Great's house, a small wooden house now built over to protect it, the best room and that in which he lived might be 16' by 16', the bed-room not half the size, it is now used by the priests, there they have a picture of a Saint before this about a score of wax candles were flaming away softened by their own combined heat, two priests were chanting, and perspiring as well they might, as if against time, 'Oh Dear' 'Oh Dear' twas said of old, 'the darkness is past', but surely darkness has come again. Near this is the font and the Church where the Imperial family is interred, here is the most prodigious gold altar screen I ever saw, it rises forty to fifty feet.

On First-day we had our receivings and sundry callers; in the evening Baron Nicholas who introduced us to the Emperor called to say we were requested to remain until Third-day as the Grand Duchess Mary wished us to call, that to make up for this delay they would give us a Government Courier having power to take horses in preference to all others, this would expedite us very much. Besides this, the Emperor wished us to have a souvenir from him, we assented to the former, and in a very civil note declined the latter knowing that if on our return home we spoke in favour of peace with R. it would be said we were bribed.

Second-day the thermometer was six below zero, in the evening we were at a large tea party, comprising many of the best English residents, kindly invited to meet us. On Third-day we called upon the Grand Duchess it was not worth the detention from the commencing of our journey. We left about five p.m. and worked on pleasantly during the night, but there was much snow and wind, and about seven a.m. we had a real roll-over, and it was a business to get clambered up through the windows as out of a well, after a while natives gathered round and 'mouth' and sinews were soon effectual, a window broken and other small damage.

Riga seventh-day, we are safe here but have had weary work with the snow, we may be in London on Sixth-day night. I will write to thee as soon as I can from there and a note to be there, Hughes, on Seventh-day will be acceptable as thine is here to-day but thy Cairn Bank news touches me very much.

I intended to have given thee a little history in this but cannot manage it, yesterday we had sixteen degrees of frost, to-day wind and snow.

Thy ever affectionate,

Henry Pease

Additional Memoranda from Robert Charleton's Diary of the Last Stages of the Journey Home

We left Dorpat on sixth day morning, Second month 17th, a little before daylight, and the state of the roads, as we advanced, plainly showed the wisdom of not encountering so much danger in the darkness of the preceding night. In one place we overtook the Malle Post stuck fast in a snowdrift, the nine horses attached to it appearing unable to drag it out. Our carriage being lighter got through more easily; but in order to accomplish this, the driver was obliged to force our seven horses into a gallop a little before reaching the obstacle, availing himself of the momentum thus acquired for dragging it through the drift. Towards evening the road became better, and we ventured to travel through the night; not, however, without much difficulty and various stoppages in the snowdrifts.

We reached Riga about noon the following day, Seventh-day, but did not stop there long as we had decided to proceed to Mitau, intending to spend First-day there. But on leaving Riga and crossing the Dwina into Courland, the weather became warmer, and the snow began so rapidly to melt, that our courier feared we were on the eve of a general thaw, which would effectually put a stop to all travelling for a time ; and in order, if possible to avoid so serious a delay, we gave up reluctantly, our intention of stopping during First-day and pushed on through the night towards Tauroggen. During the night the frost set in again, and towards morning we found the snow thicker and the roads worse than they had been at all, so that for a considerable distance our rate of travelling could not much exceed two miles an hour. After daylight things began to mend, and we enjoyed the sight of a magnificent sunrise ; the effect of which over an unbroken expanse of snow was extremely fine. Some hours later we were interested in observing the peasantry flocking to rustic looking churches (Greek) ; some walking, but most of them on light sledges of a rude construction drawn by a single horse. The effect was quite picturesque, and judging from the numbers collected from a thinly inhabited district, I should think that the habit of attending public worship among these poor people must be almost universal.

We reached Tauroggen about the middle of the day, and after spending a few hours there, in the course of which we held our little meeting, we proceeded in the evening to Tilsit, the first town in Prussia, which we reached about ten o'clock. On crossing the frontier, a few miles after leaving Tauroggen, the officer at the Prussian custom house, an agreeable old man, came to the window of our carriage, accosting us with the salutation, 'Welcome to Prussian ground, gentlemen !' Independently of this man's kind civility it was a great comfort to us to find ourselves again in Germany. We got to bed at Tilsit towards eleven o'clock ; but, although we had not been in bed before since leaving Dorpat, I found it very difficult to go to sleep, either from being too much fatigued or from the nervous system being over excited. However, we rose early the next morning, and set out in good spirits for Konigsberg, which we reached early in the evening. The day was cold, the thermometer at eight or nine o'clock a.m. being down to 15 or 16 degrees ; but the sun shone brilliantly in a cloudless sky, and there being no wind, we were not at all inconvenienced by the cold.

After staying an hour or two at Konigsberg, we proceeded by the night train for Berlin. The change from our cramped position when travelling from Petersburg to the spacious seats and soft cushions of the first class carriages on the Prussian railway, was very great and very pleasant; so we slept a great deal through the night, and a little before daylight in the morning we reached Dirschau on the left bank of the Vistula. Here we waited a considerable time, and refreshed ourselves with an early breakfast. The frost was severe and the sky remarkably clear; and in walking up and down the platform, my attention was much attracted by the sparkling brilliancy of the planet Venus, then recently risen. After a pretty long day's journey we reached Berlin about ten in the evening, and lodged at our old quarters at the Hotel de Saxe.

We left Berlin early next morning, and proceeded by way of Brunswick, Hanover, etc. to Cologne, which we reached late at night, and after procuring supper we immediately set out again for Belgium and England. The morning dawned on us a little before getting to Malines; and the mild air and the sight for the first time of green fields, were exceedingly pleasant. We had been for so long accustomed to view the unbroken expanse of snow in Russia, and the scarcely less wintry aspect of nature whilst travelling through North Germany, that the total disappearance of white, and the substitution for it of the smiling verdure of West Belgium, were extremely refreshing to us. We breakfasted at Malines, and proceeded by way of Ghent and Lille to Calais, whence we crossed to Dover and proceeded by the evening train to London, which we were favoured to reach in safety on Fifth-day evening.

We were also in good health with the exception of a heavy cold which I took, as I suppose, in consequence of our sudden transition, by the rapid railway travelling, from the frosty atmosphere to which we had so long been accustomed to the mild damp air of the English Channel. Our journey from Dorpat, about sixteen hundred miles, was performed within the week, a rate of travelling which has rarely been equalled excepting by Cabinet couriers, etc; and considering the unusual risk that we unavoidably incurred from the state of the roads in Russia, it is indeed cause for humble thankfulness to our great Preserver that we were able to accomplish this undertaking without encountering any material accident.

We lodged at W. Hughes's, and spent Sixth-day, and most of Seventh-day, in conferring with the Meeting for Sufferings and waiting on the Earl of Aberdeen. These engagements being completed, we returned to our respective homes on Seventh-day night, the 25th of Second Month.

CHAPTER IX

Home Again

THE THREE TRAVELLERS went their separate ways on Saturday, 25th February. No doubt they were thankful to be safely home again after an absence of five weeks. Less than five weeks later, on 29th March, war was declared. It was expected to be short and decisive, but the Crimean war dragged on for two years, an incredible mixture of muddle and mismanagement, bravery and heroism, with terrible suffering and loss of life on both sides. It was only after the fall of Sebastopol in the spring of 1856 that the way was opened for peace negotiations.

Joseph Sturge was very upset that his efforts to prevent war had been unsuccessful, his distress must have been increased by the press attacks on him. As a corn merchant he was especially vulnerable; he was accused of wanting peace because the war stopped his profits in Russian grain, and of conspiring with other merchants to keep up the existing high price of corn. The strain affected his health; he wrote to a friend in America:

> I am going down-hill both bodily and mentally; yet it is a cause for thankfulness that I have been permitted so long the privilege of health and strength, and a disposition to labour, however feebly, for the amelioration of human suffering and the promotion of human happiness.

Joseph Sturge spent part of the winter of 1854-5 in Torquay, where, like many people since, he found the milder climate and sea air beneficient. Slowly during the course of 1855 he recovered much of his vitality. He was able to help Bright and Cobden start the *Morning* and *Evening Star* papers, which was made possible by the repeal of the newspaper stamp tax.

On 20th March, 1856, Joseph Sturge was well enough to travel to Paris with Henry Richards and Charles Hindley M.P. to present a Memorial from the Peace Conference Committee praying that the plenipotentiaries should put into the Peace Treaty a provision binding the signatory powers to submit disputes to an impartial body of arbitrators. They did not manage to get an audience with the French Emperor Napoleon III, but they had a sympathetic reception from Lord Clarendon, the British representative. When the proceedings of the Peace Congress were published the following protocol had been drawn up and unanimously adopted;–

> The plenipotentiaries do not hesitate to express, in the name of their Governments, the wish that states, between which any serious misunderstandings may arise, should, before appealing to arms, have recourse, as far as circumstances might allow, to the good offices of a friendly power.

The idea of submitting disputes to arbitration had been advocated by Joseph Sturge since his meeting in America with Judge William Jay in 1841. William Jay was the son of the American Chief Justice John Jay, from whom the 1794 Jay Treaty acquired its name. This treaty settled frontier claims between Britain and America. Joseph Sturge printed the manuscript of a scheme which Judge William Jay had drawn up, providing for the insertion of an arbitration clause in all conventional treaties. This idea was adopted by the London Peace Society and by the International Peace Congresses of 1843 and 1848.

In 1849 Henry Cobden put the substance of it into a motion which he brought before the House of Commons, and secured, in a rather empty House, seventy-nine votes in its favour. Lord Palmerston, who was the Prime Minister at the end of the Crimean War, did not support the idea, preferring as he himself hinted, 'the dazzling results of war' to 'the solid advantages of peace'. Palmerston's great opponent Gladstone said in the House of Commons:–

> As to the proposal to submit international differences to arbitration, I think that it is in itself a very great triumph, a powerful engine on behalf of civilisation and humanity. It is, perhaps, the first time that the representatives of the principal nations of Europe have given emphatic utterance to sentiments which contain, at least, a qualified disapproval of a resort to war, and assert the supremacy of reason, of justice, humanity, and religion.

Joseph Sturge should have been pleased that he had played a part in the evolution of a great practical idea by his work in the years between 1841 and 1856. He insisted that the Peace Committee should visit Lord Clarendon in Paris, rather than accepting Lord Palmerston's rebuff which had so disheartened Cobden and most of the Peace Committee. The advantages of arbitration began to be more widely recognised, and although unfortunately not always successful in preventing major conflicts, it was a step in the right direction: a small step, which led to the setting up of the International Court of Justice at the Hague, the League of Nations at Geneva, and to the establishment of the United Nations Organisation in New York.

In September 1856 Joseph Sturge and his friend Thomas Harvey, the old companion of his West Indies tour, were off on another fact finding mission, this time to Finland. The poor defenceless Finns had been the first to suffer in the Crimean war. Even before the war started, the British Admiral Napier had boasted, at a dinner given at the Reform Club in London, that he would make the shores of the Baltic resound with deeds of naval daring. When he reached the Baltic he found that he could not attack the Russian warships or their naval bases; instead, without any apparent military reason, he carried out raids along the Finnish coast, burning fishing villages, destroying boats, nets and stores. This was wanton destruction especially as the Finns were likely to be more friendly to the English than to the Russians, who had conquered and annexed their country. The piteous condition of the Finnish inhabitants is described by a local correspondent who wrote to *The Times* in June 1854:–

The number of fugitive Finns increases here every day. Whoever walks round our harbour sees a vast number of ragged people lying about on the stones, whose nocturnal abode is the tents they have contrived to make out of tattered sails. One shriek of woe sounds all through Finland! It will be many years before those wretched outcasts regain the point which they had hitherto by great assiduity obtained. All their vessels of any size are in the hands of the English and the smaller ones are totally destroyed. All the stock of timber and pitch that they are wont to export to Denmark and even to Germany in the spring, and which constitutes their chief source of livelihood, is reduced to ashes. Anything and everything that might possibly be useful to the Russians has been destroyed.

Joseph Sturge and Thomas Harvey were only in Finland just over a fortnight, but they managed to see some of the damage done, and to set up in the old capital of Abo a local committee of merchants who undertook to administer the British relief fund. Joseph Sturge wanted to stress that there were many people in England who disapproved of the Navy's wanton destruction and that the relief was 'not an act of bounty or of mercy, but of mere justice'. The sum collected by the Committee of the Society of Friends was not large, only about £9,000, but it represented much goodwill; and was a precedent for the 'War Victims Relief Fund' which Friends have organised and administered in more recent wars, including sending relief to the Finns after their war with Russia in 1939.

In the autumn of 1856 Henry Cobden, writing about his friend, said:

It is really refreshing to see Sturge's inexhaustible energy. He could run a dozen young men off their legs. No sooner is he back from his visit to Finland than he inquires if there is nothing to be done! I

93

wonder what such men would do, if the world's crimes and follies did not find them plenty of employment in the work of well-doing.

Joseph Sturge continued his work of 'well-doing' for the rest of his life. He proposed going to India on another fact finding mission after the Indian Mutiny in 1857; but he was advised by Englishmen who knew the country that it would be impractical to try to make any fruitful inquiry for the time being. Instead Joseph Sturge accepted the post of President of the Peace Society, and spent much of his time speaking at a series of meetings in the North of England. He also helped John Bright with his election campaign in Birmingham in April 1859, and was preparing for the annual meeting of the Peace Society in May when he died. His biographer Stephen Hobhouse writes:

> He rose about six o'clock, and, after his usual time of prayer, called his little daughters to accompany his ride on their ponies. A fit of coughing came on followed by a severe heart attack. Before many minutes passed the spirit had left the body that had served it so well. The funeral took place on a day of pouring rain. Nevertheless it is said that the two miles of streets traversed were lined on either side by crowds of people. He was buried in the Friends' Burial Ground at the Birmingham Meeting House.

In June 1862 a statue was unveiled by W. Middlemore in the presence of John Bright M.P., W. Scholefield M.P. and 12,000 people. The statue was to commemorate Sturge's work as a Quaker philanthropist, worker for the abolition of slavery, and as an Alderman since 1838 in the first Borough Council of Birmingham. The memorial took the form of a statue and fountain. The inauguration was described by *The Times*:

> *The statue has been erected on by far the best site of the town; it is at one of the boundaries, where the parishes of Birmingham and Edgbaston meet, this being the parish in which Mr. Sturge resided. The monument consists of a central figure of Mr. Sturge, his right hand resting upon a Bible, and the left extended towards a figure symbolical of Peace. A figure on the other side is typical of Charity. At the base of the statue, in front and back, are large basins for ornamental fountains, and at either side are drinking fountains. The principal figure is in Sicilian marble, the secondary groups in fine freestone. The likeness of the man is portrayed with wonderful fidelity. The expressions of benevolence which spoke so powerfully in life, are depicted wonderfully in stone. The allegorical figures with their symbols, are also very cleverly executed. There was a large assembly to-day to witness the undraping of the statue; Mr. John Bright and Mr. Scholefield, the Borough members, were present as were also the Mayor and many members of the Corporation.*

94

Joseph Sturge's Statue

The statue survived the bombing of the second world war and the redevelopment of Birmingham. It has now been moved from a very busy traffic island at Five Ways, Edgbaston, to a garden site nearby.

Robert Charleton caught the Western Express from London to Bristol to return to his 'Dearest Love' and his many friends. His sister-in-law Anna Fox wrote:

> Although the pacific embassy of our friends was not crowned with success, we cannot doubt but that their Christian heroism conveyed a teaching lesson to many minds, subsequently enforced by the enormous waste of life and treasure in the Crimean war. No sentiment of regret at having borne a part in this mission of peace and goodwill was ever expressed by Robert Charleton.

He continued with his philanthropic work as before.

In the spring of 1858 Robert Charleton accompanied Josiah Forster to Paris to try to stop the slave trade, especially the importation of coolies into some of the French colonies. This time they did not shake hands with an Emperor, they only saw the Minister for Foreign Affairs. They called on the Duc de Broglie, who had been the chief Minister during Louis Philippe's reign, but now had no political influence, and met the Baroness de Stael, widow of the son of the famous Madame de Stael.

In the summer of the same year Robert Charleton was off on his travels again, this time to Russia. He accompanied Robert Forster and Francis J. Fry, as a deputation to the Governments of Northern Europe to present the 'Plea for Liberty of Conscience', issued by the Society of Friends. This summer journey was much easier, by train to Stettin and then by sea to St. Petersburg, where they settled comfortably at Benson's Hotel. They were not allowed to see the Russian Emperor, but travelled out to the Summer Palace at Peterhoff to meet Prince Gortschakoff. Robert Charleton writes:

> He showed us great courtesy and kindness, read the Address attentively, but said the circulation in Russia could not be allowed. We gave him a copy on vellum, for the Emperor, which he promised duly to present.

This business concluded, the Friends were free to enjoy some sightseeing, they visited the Wheeler cemetery at Shoosharry, and afterwards went on to Tzarsko-Selo.

> We spent two hours walking and driving about the palaces gardens and shrubberies. The beauty of these quite surprised us, and we thought them in some respects superior to the Summer Palace at Peterhoff, which we had seen the day before, notwithstanding the effect of the grand waterworks at the latter, equal to those at

Versaille, which we had the good fortune to see in full operation. But the sight of all this splendour and beauty did not remove the much stronger impressions produced on my mind by our visit to the cemetery at Shoosharry: feelings in which my companions also largely shared.

The delegation travelled by train to Moscow through 'a primeval wilderness, with the exception of small patches of cultivated land in the neighbourhood of the stations'. They returned to St. Petersburg and then on to Helsingfors and Stockholm. There the mission had more success and Robert Charleton was left with a very favourable impression of Sweden and the Swedes.

In Copenhagen they had five hundred copies of the Address printed in Danish. While there they talked to a Baptist, Parson Lassen, who traced the religious freedom which now exists in Denmark due in no small degree to the visit of Elizabeth Fry with her brother, Joseph John Gurney, in 1841. Elizabeth Fry met some Baptists in prison, and her representations to the King of Denmark led to their liberation, and some years afterwards liberty of conscience was fully established by law.

From Copenhagen the delegation travelled by train to Hamburg, a town which has suffered greatly from fires. Robert Charleton writes: 'the part of the city which was destroyed by the great conflagration of 1842 has been rebuilt on a much grander scale'. The same comment could be made today after its destruction in the second world war. The mission took them on to Mecklenburg; they intended to return via Magdeburg, but the trains on that line were not convenient so they returned via Hanover, Minden, Cologne and Calais, and home for a holiday at Torquay.

Apart from a visit to Ireland in 1864 Robert Charleton's other journeys were to attend conferences and to speak at meetings in England. He spoke at the Annual Meeting of the Peace Society, and gave a lecture on the Protestant Reformation in England. In 1860 Robert Charleton was unanimously recorded by the Monthly Meeting of Bristol as an approved Minister of the Gospel. The time he devoted to religious matters increased, although ill health resulted in more time being spent writing letters and less time travelling and making speeches.

His only son was born in 1860. Having waited so long for a child, Anna Fox writes:

. . . an event which could not but be regarded by the parents as a cause for humble and thankful rejoicing, in which many kind friends cordially shared, as well as in the desire and prayer that he might be spared to become a blessing.

He was spared until after his father's death, but sadly committed suicide. The medical evidence went to show that the serious head injury Mr. Charleton received by a fall from a bicycle in 1877 was the primary cause of the intermittent tendency to suicide. The jury returned a verdict of 'Suicide while in a state of temporary insanity'. He was mourned by his wife and mother, his father having died in 1872 after a long and painful illness.

The Times reported on 12th July, 1872:

> A peacemaker, Mr. Robert Charleton, a distinguished member of the Society of Friends, died yesterday at his residence, Ashley Down, Bristol. Mr. Charleton, it will probably be remembered, was one of the deputation of three members of the Society of Friends who proceeded from this country to Russia to endeavour to dissuade the Emperor from prosecuting the Crimean War. He was a gentleman of large property, a very great portion of the income derived from which he devoted to benevolent purposes. He was the son of an old Bristol merchant, Mr. James Charleton, who carried on business as a sugar refiner. The deceased was a prominent member of the Peace Society; he took a conspicuous part in the operations of the Anti-Slavery Society, was one of the foremost advocates of the Temperance movement in the West of England and was strongly in favour of the adoption of the Permissive Liquor Bill. The deceased was aged 64.

There was also a long account of his life and work in the local papers, the same journals which had poured scorn on his peace making efforts and his journey to visit the Czar of Russia nearly twenty years earlier.

Henry Pease returned to Darlington, where on 18th March he gave a public lecture. *The Times* reported that the Central Hall, the largest room in the town, was crowded to excess in every part, and there could not have been less than 2,000 persons present.

> Mr. Pease said that he could not help feeling that that large audience had been brought together by the unusual degree of interest now manifested in Russia. He proceeded to give some interesting details of what happened to the deputation on their journey, and their encounters with the officials at the several places through which they passed. He said he took no credit to himself as having done some great thing in performing this journey of 2,000 miles. Arrived at the palace of the Czar, he described the magnificence of the palace and the gracious reception accorded them by the Emperor. The Address which the deputation presented and the reply of the Czar had already been published

There was, he thought, nothing unreasonable or anything to ridicule in a body of men who had been in existence for 200 years, who had always believed that the disputes of nations could never be settled by appealing to the sword, sending three of their number to endeavour to bring about a pacific settlement of the dispute, without appealing to such an awful thing as war.

He had brought with him a tattered portion of an illustrated paper which had been mutilated in its passage through the post office, and all the articles which were not considered by the authorities to be respectable were cut away. He ascribed the little or no progress which Russia made in civilization to the fettering of the press in that country.

The Emperor, he said, seemed to be fully aware of the state of public opinion in this country with reference to the Eastern question. Both the Czar himself and other members of the Imperial family, to whom the deputation were introduced, carefully abstained from making any allusion to the articles which the newspaper press in England continued to publish about the late aggression. Mr. Pease said that no one cherished more ardently than himself the love for the freedom of the press in England, but he was exceedingly grieved and humbled at the course which the press in England had pursued in reference to this Eastern question, in resorting to abuse and calumny against the Czar, instead of reasoning calmly and appealing to sound judgement. He could not believe but that the impressions which were conveyed to the public through the press were entirely erroneous and unfounded as regards the Emperor and Empress. The effect which these misrepresentations had on the minds of both were painfully apparent. He did not give this as his own opinion merely, but many of the most respectable British residents in St. Petersburg were of the same opinion, and expressed their sorrow to the deputation at the course pursued by the press in this country. From what he saw of the Emperor and Empress he was convinced that the estimation in which the former was held here was incorrect. He believed that the Czar was kind and temperate. His own people were devoted to him, and he very often went out among them unguarded, when he was always received with great enthusiasm.

The speaker said the river commanding a view of St. Petersburg was very strongly fortified indeed. He characterised war as inhuman, unnatural, and unreasonable, and expressed his conviction that after thousands of lives had been sacrificed the question would remain precisely where it now was.

99

Mr. Pease was heartily cheered during the evening, but the majority of the audience seemed much disappointed that more reference had not been made to the present aspect of the Eastern question. A vote of thanks to the speaker closed the proceedings.

Henry Pease made other journeys and other speeches in the cause of peace. In 1867 he was one of a deputation from the London Peace Society to visit the Emperor Louis Napoleon to ask for his permission to hold an International Peace Congress in Paris at the time of the Exhibition. The Emperor received them in the Palace of the Tuileries. The reception was civil but the request was refused.

On Henry Pease's next visit to Paris in 1871, the Emperor Louis Napoleon was in exile in England, after the French defeat in the Franco-Prussian war, and the Tuileries Palace was in ruins. Henry Pease stood among the ruins and looked up through the charred beams to the blackened walls, which were all that remained of the sumptuous room where he had stood face to face with the Emperor three years before. Mary Pease in her biography of her husband says that:

> As he gazed at the broken disfigured trees and other marks of desolation and destruction, he thought that it was an eloquent commentary on the cruel uncertainties and miseries of war.

An International Peace Congress was held in Paris in 1878 which Henry Pease attended. He had been President of the Peace Society since his brother Joseph's death in 1872. He also followed in his brother Joseph's footsteps by becoming the Liberal Member of Parliament for South Durham in 1857. Joseph as the first Quaker M.P. had met with a great deal of opposition and criticism even from some of his own family, but Henry's decision was accepted by his father Edward Pease who wrote: 'I have always liked Christian men being sent to the House of Commons'.

This passage from Henry's electoral address gives some idea of his main interests.

> I was born and have lived among you. I have associated with you in every walk of life, and whether for commercial or railway enterprises, in struggles for political reform and general education, in the service of science or philanthropy, you know I have not shrunk from work. If, however, instead of cordial co-operation with you at home, I am to serve you in a more extensive sphere elsewhere, I feel no doubt that my long cherished local friendships, and my known love for South Durham, will afford you sufficient guarantees that your interest will ever occupy my earnest attention.

Henry Pease was fortunate to be in Parliament at a time when there were several very interesting characters in the House. Palmerston was a veteran statesman, Mr. Disraeli and Mr. Gladstone were carrying on their long Parliamentary duel, while John Bright was at the zenith of his powers, electrifying the House with his speeches. But Henry did not enjoy city life, so that he was pleased to relinquish his seat in 1865, being succeeded by his nephew. It seems incredible that even after the passing of the 1832 Parliamentary Reform Act a seat could be held by one family for so long.

Henry had another reason for giving up his seat in Parliament; he wanted to be able to spend more time at home with his wife and young family. He had married Mary Lloyd, daughter of Samuel and Mary Lloyd, of Woodgreen Wednesbury, on 19th January, 1859. Unfortunately Edward Pease died a few months before his son's second marriage, as he had hoped his son would remarry, and even spent some time trying to find him a suitable wife. Edward wrote in his diary in 1847: 'Went to London to see Robert Barcley on my dear son Henry's account, had an agreeable interview and obtained for him all I could wish, that he might see Jane Mary'. Henry called, but nothing came of this meeting, Jane Mary died a spinster aged 81 in 1899. Perhaps he had already lost his heart to Mary Lloyd when she went to tea at Pierremont while staying with cousins in Darlington. At first it seemed as if his cause was hopeless, but in the end Henry's determination overcame Mary's fears and in spite of the difference in age, between 32 and 50, they appear to have been very happy with a large family of three sons and two daughters. His youngest daughter Marion wrote:

For a daughter to speak of such a loved father is difficult, and to us his memory seems all that was noble and beautiful. We shall always remember his courteous tenderness to our mother and his tender love to us his children. He was swift with righteous anger for anything he thought mean or wrong, but gentle with sensitive kindness and tact to the weak or sorrowful. He was a most genial, kind host, and loved to show hospitality to relations and friends.

An extract from a Jubilee Memorial written in 1875 gives some idea of his work and interest in his native town:

He has distinguished himself more than any other gentleman in Darlington or its neighbourhood for his horticultural taste and his gardens at South Pierremont are hardly to be rivalled at Chatsworth or Studley Royal. Like his father before him he has a remarkable love of trees, and has spent much money in beautifying some of the principal thoroughfares of Darlington by planting them in such a way as will in the course of a few years give the roads the appearance of Boulevards.

He was made first Mayor of Darlington in 1867 and held the position for two years, furnishing to the deliberations of the new Council that high and dignified nature which is so essentially part of his own nature.

Henry Pease continued to work for the benefit of local people, taking a special interest in education and welfare. He gave his time and money generously to his fellow citizens, always prepared to help when help was needed. Darlington was not the only town to benefit from his philanthropy. In 1859 he discovered Saltburn, then a small fishing village on the Yorkshire coast, which he decided to develop as a seaside resort, not just for the rich, but for the workers of Middlesbrough and Stockton. He first built a railway, which provided cheap and easy travel for people who had not been able to have holidays before. As well as houses and hotels, he built and endowed a Convalescent Home so that those in greatest need could enjoy the sea air. His plans included a promenade and pier and the public gardens, which still stand as a monument to his genius.

But perhaps the legacy which would have pleased him most are his many descendants; his daughter Marion Fox writing in 1938 said: 'Our parents had 22 grandchildren, there are 37 great grandchildren living'. Now as one of the great grandchildren writing in 1984, I know there are many great-great grandchildren, and at least 15 great-great-great grandchildren alive today, some of whom may be interested to read about their ancestor's peace mission to the Czar.

Meeting for Sufferings tried to keep in touch with the deputation while they were away, and to publish the Address and the reply when they returned. At their meeting, held the third of the second month 1854, there is a minute recorded that:

Report is made that our friends Joseph Sturge and Robert Charleton accompanied by Henry Pease, who was selected to that service agreeable to the discretion given to the Committee, as a deputation appointed to proceed to Petersburg to present the Address to the Emperor of Russia, left London on 20th of last month intending to proceed by way of Berlin, and that intelligence has been received of them from Konigsberg on the 25th ultimo.

As soon as the deputation returned to London a special Meeting for Sufferings was held on 25th of 2nd month, convened at the requisition of its members. The minute records:

This meeting has been specially summoned to receive the deputation appointed to present to the Emperor of Russia the Address of the Society of Friends on the subject of war. The deputation being present have given to the Meeting some interesting particulars of their proceedings and have presented a reply to the said Address signed by Count Nesselrode the Chancellor of the Empire, on behalf of the Emperor. This meeting feels thankful for the Providential care extended towards our dear friends in their arduous journey, and that the way has so satisfactorily opened for accomplishing the service committed to them. It is concluded after deliberation to publish the Address and the reply, together with such other information of the proceedings as may seem expedient to the committee before appointed, who are continued to attend the same.

The minute for the third month records:

The committee on the circulation of the Address to the Emperor of Russia are continued. The Address to the Emperor of Russia and his answer to be sent to Dublin Yearly Meeting.

At the next Meeting for Sufferings held 7th of 4th month 1854 the minute reads:

The committee on the presentation and circulation of the Address to the Emperor of Russia report that their duties in connexion with this service have been attended to.

The final duty of Meeting for Sufferings was to report to London Yearly Meeting. Robert Charleton in a letter written from London on 5th month 31 states:

The minutes of the Meeting for Sufferings relating to our mission to Petersburg, and also the report of that visit, with pretty much in way of verbal addition from Joseph Sturge, occupied the greatest part of another sitting. Friends generally expressed satisfaction with the concern of the Meeting for Sufferings in this affair, and also in the manner in which the deputation had carried it out.

This would be as much praise as any of the Friends would expect. As the Crimean war had already begun, Yearly Meeting was now concerned with issuing some kind of document on the Testimony of Friends against war.

Charleton writes: 'There was some interesting discussion on this subject, and I believe it will also be referred to in the Yearly Meeting Epistle'. He concludes one of his letters with: 'On the whole Y.M. has been probably as interesting and instructive as any for a number of years'.

The Friend in its account of Yearly Meeting printed in June wrote:

Third-day afternoon, the greater part of this sitting was occupied with the subject of the mission of our Friends Joseph Sturge, Henry Pease and Robert Charleton, to the Emperor of Russia. It was introduced by reading the minute of the Meeting for Sufferings, and the printed account of our Friend's journey and reception at St. Petersburg. Joseph Sturge then gave a lengthened and very interesting report of the proceedings of the deputation, and the course adopted by the Meeting for Sufferings and the manner in which the deputation had executed their mission received the cordial approval of the Meeting.

Samuel Gurney reported the interview with the Foreign Secretary, Lord Clarendon, when our Friends had left the country for Russia, and of their interview with the Prime Minister, Lord Aberdeen, on their returning to this country, both of which had been very satisfactory.

One or two Friends, W. T. Clayton and W. Fowler, expressed some regret, that none of the deputation should, since their return, have expressed their opinions of the personal character of the Emperor of Russia, a subject on which there was a decided difference of sentiment, and which was not connected with the simple testimony to the evils and iniquity of all war.

John Bright expressed very strongly his opinion, that the appointment of the deputation was a right step, and he believed the Friends had most efficiently and satisfactorily fulfilled the duty to which they had devoted themselves. He expressed himself personally obliged to the friends for the way in which they had performed their service. He alluded to the Earl of Aberdeen, and said he was convinced that the Premier had been from the first most anxious to avoid the war, and was still disposed to entertain favourably any proposals for an armistice, preparatory to a more lasting peace; but much was to be done to prepare the minds of the people of this country for the acceptance of equitable proposals of this character, and he urged upon Friends to use their influence in their respective localities with the newspaper press, to induce a more moderate tone in their articles on the war.

This appears to be the only occasion when John Bright, the foremost Quaker pacifist of the day gave his support to the deputation; at the time of their journey, when they were attacked by the press there was no word of encouragement. John Bright M.P. became the war's most eloquent opponent both inside and outside the House of Commons. As a Pacifist he was so unpopular in his constituency of Manchester that he was burnt in effigy.

In the Commons he was such a brilliant speaker that his speeches were admired even by his opponents. One of his most famous anti-war speeches was on 23rd February, 1855 when he said:

The Angel of Death has been abroad throughout the land; you may almost hear the beating of his wings. There is no one, as when the first born were slain of old to sprinkle with blood the lintels and side posts of our doors, that he may spare us and pass on; he takes his victims from the castle of the noble, the mansion of the wealthy, and the cottage of the poor and lowly, and it is on behalf of all these classes that I make this solemn appeal.

G. M. Trevelyan in his life of John Bright writes:

To attack the justice and wisdom of a popular war while it is still in progress requires more courage than any other act in a political society that has outgrown the assassin's dagger and the executioner's block. And it requires not only most courage but most power and skill. To perform it well is not only the rarest but one of the most valuable of public services, because to arraign an unjust and unwise war is the only way to prevent another.

Bright and Cobden, by speaking out so that they were heard against the Crimean War, while it was yet in progress, were believed when it was over. In this way they did much to prevent England from taking part in the wars of the next twenty years, in every one of which she had as much concern as in the Eastern question of 1854.

Had it not been for the lesson which Bright now began to teach in circumstances so unpleasant to himself, it is not improbable that we should have fought for Austria against France in 1859, or for the slave owners against the North in 1861, or for Denmark against Germany in 1864, or again for Turkey against Russia in 1878. And if we had entered into any one of these wars, or into the Franco-German war of 1870, very little more would have been heard of the famous Victorian prosperity.

Joseph Sturge, Robert Charleton and Henry Pease were unable to prevent the Crimean War, but the Quaker influence for Peace and their efforts to bind up the wounds of war, played a significant part in the history of Britain; so that they and their families and other Quaker Industrialists were able to contribute to, and enjoy, the benefits from the 'Famous Victorian prosperity'.

Catherine Charleton's Desk

Appendix I

Letter from Robert Charleton to his brother, James Hale Charleton

PENZANCE 7TH MO 14TH 1830

My Dear Brother,

Thy letter dated 26th: of last month, though for some cause, considerably delayed on the road, not arriving here for more than a week after the time of it's date, was very acceptable to me, more especially as I had been rather anxiously expecting to hear from you for a considerable time previous to its arrival.

I am glad to hear that our dear Father enjoys a comfortable state of health, please give my dear love to him, inform him that I shall be much pleased to receive a few lines from him, when it may be convenient to him to write.

James Ireland Wright arrived here with his son, last sixth day morning, they quickly hired a conveyance and visited the Logan Rock, Lands End, and Botallock Mine, to which places I accompanied them. The time was short but the weather fine, I believe they were pleased with their excursions. James Wright informed me that Edward was likely to be with them in the business, I should think that it would be a comfortable situation for him in many respects.

16th; Not having been able to make a finish of my letter on third day evening, I again put pen to paper for that purpose, although with very little prospect of being able to communicate anything interesting. Letter writing is quite a task, although it might be supposed that in corresponding with one so near as a brother, no great difficulty need be experienced. I feel sorry, I did not request thee, before thy leaving Penzance, to give me some account of the proceedings at the Yearly Meeting. It appears from what I have heard of it to have been a highly instructive and interesting occasion. John Dymond of Exeter, called and took tea here this evening. This being the day, on which the remains of our late King are to be interred, business has been mostly suspended, we have been further reminded of it this evening, by the firing of minute guns on board of the Revenue Cruiser.

Business in our line is at present very slack and dull, so that we are obliged to discharge our men, and give them such occasional work as we can find for them. The weather has been very variable here; with little continuance of the hot summer weather; I understand, however, the crops promise fair, excepting potatoes, of which there appears to be a failure in some places.

J.S. and wife desire their love to you.

Please give my love to Aunt Bonville, Aunt Hunt, and Br. Edward, as thee mayst have opportunity. Hoping to hear from thee before very long.

I remain thy affectionate Br.

Robert Charleton

Letter from Robert Charleton to Catherine Brewster Fox
a few months before their marriage

IN LONDON 4 MONTH 17TH 1849

My beloved Friend,

I came here this morning on Trade business, I expect to return to Bristol tomorrow. I am glad I did not leave home yesterday, or I should have missed thy letter which met me in the evening at Ashley Hill. Thou speaks of thy letters being written in a somewhat 'cold and cautious' manner; but, be this as it may, they have all been most welcome to my feelings. The prudence – the delicacy of feeling – and the correct and enlightened views on the important subject before us, displayed in thy letters, and practically exhibited in thy conduct towards me when I was at Rushmere, have made a very powerful impression upon me. I am not surprised that thou shouldst consider my affection for thee as resting on the basis of a comparatively slight acquaintance. But though it is common to speak of love as blind, yet I presume it may be more discriminating, and without meaning to lay claim to any unusual share of penetration, I do say, that the insights which thou hast, perhaps unintentionally, given me into thy feelings and character, renders me more than satisfied with the choice I have been led to make. A more decided expression of reciprocal feeling would of course, have been grateful; but for this I am content to wait, feeling assured that if the proceeding be a right one, it will come in due time.

I entirely concur in thy view of the division of Society into different classes being a providential arrangement – and that, whilst the comforts and accommodation enjoyed by each respectively should be, to a considerable extent, proportioned to their means; it is important to guard against luxury, extravagance, and display, as among the worst foes to

108

health, mental serenity, and domestic happiness. The views inculcated by our Society with regard to 'Simplicity and Moderation' are precisely those which I should be led to act on, from a conviction of their tendency to promote real happiness – irrespectively of the question of moral or religious obligation.

My own preference would be for about such a style of living and scale of expenditure as that adopted by my dear Parents, in bringing up their family; which practically embraces all the comforts, excluding, for the most part, the luxuries referred to. I presume that such a mode of living would not be dissimilar from that to which thou hast been accustomed, and which thy present inclination would lead thee to select. I feel thankful in being able to state that my present income would be sufficient to meet the expenses of such an establishment, at least for some time to come, without any very material curtailment of the sum which I have been accustomed to devote to other objects. Should these expenses, hereafter, be greatly increased, we must of course be guided by the dictates of prudence in this, as in all other matters. I use the pronoun 'we', for there is something to my mind inexpressibly delightful, in the prospect of having thee associated with myself in these arrangements,. I regard it as an important element in the happiness of the conjugal union, that there may be such a community, such an identity of interest and feeling between the married pair, as practically to get rid of the distinctions of 'mine' and 'thine', and that each party may feel, that in promoting the interest and welfare of the other, he is most efficiently securing his own. Such a state of things as this, is clearly implied in the terms, 'and the twain shall be one flesh', and also in the exhortation of the Apostle, that Husbands shall love their Wives, 'even as their own bodies'. What can be more attractive than the representations of such happiness when heightened and refined by the controlling influence of practical religion!

It is quite time for me to bring this long letter to a close, but before doing so I will just say that if thou shouldst feel inclined to favour me with a few lines in reply, I should feel greatly obliged by thy doing so on 5th day, so that I may get it at Ashley Hill on 6th day evening. On 2nd, 3rd and 4th days in next week, I expect to be absent, being one of the Representatives to attend the General Meeting for Sidcot School which will be held next week.

Believe me to remain,

Thine very affectionately,

Robert Charleton

Appendix II

Family Pedigree written by James Charleton

James Charleton, son of Robert Charleton and Sarah Hale, Elizabeth Ash, daughter of Edward Ash and Elizabeth Beck, were married at Bristol 5 Mo.10th 1808.

James Charleton (second time) married to Elizabeth Fox, daughter of Thomas Fox and Sarah Smith of Wellington, Somerset , 5th Mo.6th 1835.

James Charleton born 12 Mo.18 1780.

Elizabeth Charleton born 7 Mo.31 1784, died 6th Mo.29 1826 at Penzance and interred at Marazion 7th Mo.2nd aged nearly 42 years.

Eliz (Fox) Charleton born 4 Mo.19 1793.

Children of James Charleton and Elizabeth Ash.

    Robert Charleton born 4 Mo.15 1809.

    James Hale Charleton born 5 Mo.28 1811

    Edward Ash Charleton born 9 Mo.21 1815

James and Edward left Bristol 10 Mo.2nd 1836 in the Osprey Steamer for Liverpool and sailed from thence on the 15th or 16th of that month for New York.

It pleased Divine Providence, whose ways are inscrutable, to permit the ship Bristol on board of which were my dear sons James Hale and Edward Ash Charleton, to be wrecked on the 21st of the 11th Month 1836 near Sandy Hook about thirty miles from New York, their destined port. May it also have pleased our Heavenly Father to grant unto their souls an entrance through the pearl gates, into the Celestial City.

The body of J.H.C. was found on the 10th of 12th Month 1836 and conveyed to New York where it was interred in Friends' burial ground on the 13th.

The body of E.A.C. was not found until the 22nd of 1st Month 1837; it was conveyed to New York and interred on the 28th in the same grave with that of his brother.

Charleton Family Pedigree from information supplied by
James Charleton

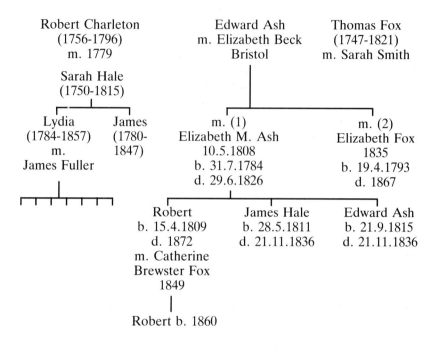

Robert Charleton
(1756-1796)
m. 1779

Sarah Hale
(1750-1815)

Edward Ash
m. Elizabeth Beck
Bristol

Thomas Fox
(1747-1821)
m. Sarah Smith

Lydia
(1784-1857)
m.
James Fuller

James
(1780-
1847)

m. (1)
Elizabeth M. Ash
10.5.1808
b. 31.7.1784
d. 29.6.1826

m. (2)
Elizabeth Fox
1835
b. 19.4.1793
d. 1867

Robert
b. 15.4.1809
d. 1872
m. Catherine
Brewster Fox
1849

James Hale
b. 28.5.1811
d. 21.11.1836

Edward Ash
b. 21.9.1815
d. 21.11.1836

Robert b. 1860

Appendix III

Among Robert Charleton's letters are several from Skaneatles, in New York State in America, where his Aunt and Uncle James and Lydia Fuller lived. From these letters it appears that he had his Uncle's power of attorney to deal with any family property or business affairs in England. After his Uncle's death he seems to have given some financial help to his cousins. He also helped settlers from Bristol who wanted to start a new life in America. Families, who found it difficult to get work in England and were prepared to risk the dangerous Atlantic crossing, often in appalling conditions, hoped to be able to make a better life for themselves in the New World. Both these letters show how hard these people worked, but how grateful they were to Robert Charleton for his kindness.

The first letter is from William Woodruff. Addressed to Robt. Charleton Esq., Kingswood Hill, Nr. Bristol, Gloucestershire, England. It is date stamped from Skaneatles N.Y. but the date is illegible; however, the Bristol date stamp is for AP 10 1848.

SKANEATLES FEB 26TH/48

Sir and Friend,

A few evenings ago my daughter told me that you had never received a letter from me since I left home. This news both surprised and grieved me, surprised that a letter duly directed and paid for should not find its destiny, and grieved lest you should charge me with ingratitude.

I wrote to you on the first post after my arrival, and it should have left Boston on the 1st. of Dec./46. I wrote to my wifes relations by the same post which they received on Christmas day.

In that letter I told you at some length of my dangerous voyage; of the storms, two of which were complete hurricanes, in which we lost 5 pieces of sail and our main mast split. I told you too of seeing the Europe, the ship I had taken passage in, but was providentially disappointed, I say I saw this ship a complete wreck in one of these gales on the banks of Newfoundland.

I told you of the good reception we met with from H. Browne and of our good health after a sickly journey. I wrote you again in the May following, in which I told you I could not get work at hatting as no hatts is made here in the winter on account of the severity of the weather. I likewise told you I had spent most of the winter in the forest cutting down trees and chopping them up into firewood mostly up to my knees and sometimes waste high in snow. But on the 26th, day of Feb, I got work in the woolen cloth factory and both my boys. My wages is 15 dollars per month. My wife now acted the part of a true helpmate turning out to washing for which she has got great credit and good wages. Thus by our joint endeavours we was enabled to send more than 100 Dollars home to bring out Henery and Eliza and her husband and child. Henery and Eliza's husband soon got work with us in the factory at 15 dollars each. But through a change in the machinery the whole four of them was discharged about Christmas and dont expect to go on again till about April. My wife has been working with me since the middle of Nov. and gets 10 Dollars per month. We have to go a mile every morning to work before 5 o'clock sometimes knee deep in snow. But for all that we are all healthy and thankfull. My tongue nor pen cannot describe mine as well as the boys and my wifes thankfullness to you Sir for sending us from a land of poverty to one of comparative plenty, for I can truly say that allthough being strangers and the boys unfortunately getting out of work, we have not wanted one meal of good substantial food since we have been here. Nor do I owe one penny to any man in this place. Mr. J. Fuller lent me 30 Dollars to help me to send to England. Which I duly paid him in one month according to our appointment.

Just before his death he sent for me to sell me a house and offered to give me six years to pay for it in. But at that time I had to work 18 hours per day and consequently could not find time to wait on him and the next news I heard of his death. Harriet sent for my wife on the last day of his life. But she was at work and did not know till the morning when he was no more. She went and stayed with them 3 days. But she being present and having to wait on the doctors at the opening of his body, was a stroke to great for her. She was obliged to return home very ill and could not be present on the day of the funeral. This great and good man is much missed and much regretted in the whole Township.

Wood for fuel is very dear and house rent is as dear as in Bristol. But all, but a few immigrants lately arrived, have houses of their own, and every poor man has an easy way to keep a cow and his hogs which give his family plenty of butter and milk and a barrel or two of pork laid up for the winter. Land is pretty cheap and easily taken up at about 40 to 50 Dollars per acre here, and further from town is to be bought for 20 Dollars and in the Western States can be bought from 2 to 10 Dollars, or a farm with a house and stable and barn etc for 20 Dollars per acre.

Now I want about as much money as I had when I left home and I could get land enough to support my family and keep myself comfortable in my old years without being obliged to labour in factorys as I find it too much for my constitution. I have paid 60 Dollars rent for the last year but have to leave it soon as it is to be sold. I had a good large garden and choice fruit and more than 100 sacks of apples, they dont sell for scarcely anything. I was advised by my neighbours to make them into Cyder and had the reproach of some for not doing it. It would have only cost two shillings per barrel and would have amounted to enough to pay my whole years rent. But I am a Teetotaller to my very backbone and would not sacrifice my principles for the gain. Besides I well remember the pit from where I have been dug and your benevolent hand in extricating me and the idea of it being a temptation to any branch of my family. I have got 50 sacks of them in the cellar where all the children have free access and they make their Cyder just when their appetites serve, and myself and wife take a great many of them to the Factory and they serve us for both meat and drink. I have got three good store pigs which have eaten about 50 sacks mixed with Indian corn meal. I have this week killed two of them and put them in barrells in the Cellar and intend to keep them there until next summer when I shall have some good pork instead of Cyder.

The Yankee's is generally a very temperate people and a great many of them is pledged members. There is a Society here called the Sons of Temperance they number 50,000 strong and each district has its branch or division. This division here has about 120 members. Myself and Henery thinks to enter it. Each division has its own local law but subject to one general law. The head quarters is I think in Washington it is called the Washingtonian Society.

Most of the intemperate people here is from England or Ireland and they very much disgrace the country they come from. Three of them have died within the last year awfully drunk all of them from the old country.

And now my dear Sir before I close I humbly hope you will send me a line in answer as I long to hear from you and the temperance cause generally. We are all tolerable well in health, yet feel myself rather too old for the extremitys of North America. My Wifes health is better than it has been for many years and she heartily joins with me in thanking you a thousand times for transporting us where the children may do for themselves in case of my or my wifes failure.

Myself and Wifes sincere respects to Mrs. Fuller and Son and Daughter. We have heard that she dont think to return again. If so and she should break up housekeeping. My wife would thank her to instruct Harriet to give her any left off clothing which would be servicable to make up for the children.

H. Browne is gone into the State of Indianna about 600 miles and has bought 20 acres of land I think for about 2 Dollars an acre.

As well as the long letters there is a short note dated Oct 1 49.

Dear Sir and Esteemed Friend

I have paid 15 Dollars over to Mrs. Fuller, and she has autherised me to request you to advance it to my Mother-in-law Elizabeth Hibbs of Frampton. I was with Mrs. Fuller yesterday afternoon, All well in health going to write to you today.

My heartfelt thanks for favours,

I remain yours W. Woodruff

The second letter is from Ham and Eliza Browne from Randolph County, Indiana, written a year later. It is a most interesting account of their difficulties in settling in Randolph County. It is addressed to Robert Charleton, Two Mile Hill, Near Kingswood, Glostershire, Near Bristol, England. It is date stamped RICHMOND IND FEB 27. and 2 AP 49 LIVERPOOL SHIP the Bristol stamp is rather smudged but it looks like AP 3 1849.

The handwriting in these letters, although very neat, is not as easy to decipher as Robert Charleton's; but I have tried to copy them as accurately as possible including, in some places, the rather quaint English and odd spelling.

Letter from Ham and Eliza Browne to Robert Charleton

RANDOLPH COUNTY INDIANA 1849 22 2 MO

Dear Robert Charleton,

I think I have greatly omited my duty in not wrighting to thee as in our last interview thou desiredst me to wright often, we wrote to thee just as we arrived at Skaneatles, it would afford us much pleasure to receive a letter from thee, we often had the pleasure to hear of thee by enquiring of thy Aunt Fuller when we lived near her which was about 2 years. It might be interesting to thee to know after I had been there

115

about 4 weeks I accidently met with my first cousin Joseph Brown with his wife and 4 children, a man greatly beloved by his neighbours, and of high standing in the Methodist Connection he had been living in Skaneatles about 5 years on his own place and in profitable employ in a large wollen Factory as Boys Fuller. I knew he was in America but did not know what part, we think a good deal of each other and since we have been in Indiana, he and his Son has come out to see us and returned Home with very favourable impressions of the Country we have some hopes he will come and settle amongst us. Thy cousin Sumner Fuller visited us several times while we were in Richmond. We were sorry to hear tell of thy Fathers decease and also of the sudden death of thy Uncle James C Fuller we felt very sorry for thy Aunt being in England at the time.

I have had the pleasure to go to several Temperance meetings with thy Uncle.

Dear Friend I would like to express my gratitude to thee for thy kindness to Wm Woodruff and his Family, they came to us on the 7th of 11th month which was a very dull time for employment we were very glad we were able to entertain them all which we did with Board for about 3 weeks till our cousin got them into employment under him and we gave them house room free of charge till the first of 4 month, our brother-in-law and David Short came with them and stayed with us all the winter so that our family was pretty large. Wm Woodruff continues in his employment but all his boys one after another has been discharged. We left before Henry arrived but we heard he had a profitable employ after leaving the factory but was discharged with the character of a thief all over the neighbourhood and being ashamed to stay there he said he would come to us, his Father enquired of my Cousin the best way for him to come. Our Friends there wrote to apprise us of his intentions and to beg us if we valued our own character and peace of mind not to admit him into our family, saying in the first place he was a common swearer and in no way fit to be amongst our children. His father has written to us twice, he wants to come here to get him a piece of land we respect him very much but fear to encourage him on account of his family. My wifes sister and 4 children has crossed the Atlantic and are at Skaneatles and intends to come to us in the Spring, there is a good many families come to that place from Winterbourn and Frampton and I hear more are coming. I feel glad that so many poor Familys are making an effort to come to this country as they can do so much better here than there.

Dear Friends I have delayed writing since the above for 3 days on account of a visit by Henry Woodruff he looks very well and very

116

smartly clothed. We were glad to hear him say he should not like to live where we do, and that he should return to an employment he had in Dayton working for a Gas Company at a Dollar per day 60 miles distant, he showed us a big handfull of money and talked very large he stayed with us one day and night and then I accompanied him 12 miles on his way back, saying he should visit us again in the Summer and that his father should certainly come this way soon to get some land.

But to proceed with my subject, in this Western part of the Country provision is much cheapest and would be the best for poor families to settle in. We left New York State on the 8 month 1847 with our own horse and waggon and arrived in Richmond in 2 weeks and five days a distance of 600 miles. We stayed in Richmond 5 weeks and then fixed on a place 60 miles North of it to live where we went but found it would not suit. So we returned back to Randolph County 25 miles North of Richmond where we now live in a settlement of Friends from North Carolina. They are a very homely people and in very middling circumstances but kind and obliging all having farms with little improvements this being a new country and mostly woods.

My dear Friend I have the satisfaction to inform thee that a little before we came into this settlement I and my wife requested membership for ourselves and all our children in the Society of Friends and are accepted by them. We are living right opposite the Friends Meeting part of which is appropriated for a weekday school room which makes it very convenient for us having so many little children. It is not kept steady only 3 months in the winter and 3 in the summer, there are 2 teachers, women Friends, this winter we have had to pay 1 Dollar ½ each child for a term. Ours so much need schooling that we have sent the five eldest that was all our family when we left England but since we have been in America we have another little girl and boy our little girl is near 3 years old, we call her Lydia Mary after thy dear Aunt Fuller and my Wife's Mother, our little son is one year old this month we call him Reuben Ham. On this spot we have bought forty acres of woodland with a deadening of 10 acres which we have cleared fenced and cropt last Summer. and built a log House on it which we live in. My house and other improvements are well nigh paid for and I have 3 years from last 4th Mo to pay for my land the price of it is one hundred and ninety Dollars. I have 2 years to make the first payment of one hundred Dollars. We have 5 acres of wheat which looks well but our stock only consists of a cow and large steer calf 18 pigs and some poultry. We met with a bad loss the first week we came here our horse ran away from us. We traced her in a North course 12 miles the same day and could never hear any more of her tho' Edgar and myself have hunted for her 14 days. I might have

117

sold her for 60 Dollars this misfortune has proved us a great hinderance on our new place as we have not been able since to buy another but intend to try to get one in the Spring. We have a nice little one horse waggon which we travelled in. I have hired a good deal of my improvements and paid for it in my trade as money is scarce in this place people expect to pay for their shoe work in labor. I have not taken five Dollars in cash in this settlement since I lived here but we can get most kind of food and clothing for shoe work in this state of things it would be impossible for me to pay for my land as I have to do it in cash. So I have taken to work out from home at Friends Houses nearer to Richmond where people mostly pay me cash for my work. It is customary here for people to find their own leather and they appear glad to have me come and make their boots and shoes and recommend me from one to another, since I have worked so I have taken about forty dollars. We think that this part of the country will

soon be better as there is a railroad about to be made through it we expect it to run about half a mile from us we shall then have a good market at a considerable town 5 miles from us called Winchester it is to run from Belfountain in Ohio to Indianappolis in this State. There are a very few Friends in this part of the country from England one from Bristol by the name of Joseph Wilmott that was intimately acquainted with my Wifes Father. We attended the Yearly Meeting of Friends held at White Water in Wayne County Indiana 9 month 1848 which was very large and I had the pleasure to dine with Benjamin Seebhoam and Robert Lindsey of Bridge House Monthly Meeting and York Quarterly Meeting England it was very pleasant to me to meet with somebody that knew thee Benjamin desired me when I wrote to thee to give his kindest love to thee. I would like to be remembered to Edward Thomas and John Ashton, I would like all my Temperance Friends to know that I and all my family is as staunch in the cause of Teetotalism as ever, the people here are generally sober, but tis a great Apple Country and some indulge a little in drinking Cyder. I should feel much pleasure if it were convenient to thee to receive the Bristol Herald I used to get a sight of it sometimes when I was at Skaneatles.

Dear Friend if by chance thee should see my parents I would take it kind of thee to tell them we were all well when this letter left us I wrote to them in the 11 Mo. When they wrote to me they told me times had been so bad there that none of the people who owed me money had been able to pay them tho' they promised me and them they would do so if they had my parents would have paid some debts I owed. Neither has it yet been my power to send any when it is I mean to do so.

My Son Edgar is grown very much and is nearly as big as myself and desires me to remember him to thee Agnes also wishes her kind love to be sent to thee we would desire to be kindly remembered to thy Aunt Fuller and thy Cousins. And now dear Robert be pleased to accept our kindest feelings to thyself and believe us to be thine most affectionately, Ham and Eliza Brown.

PS Should thee feel disposed to favour us with a letter as I hope thee will please address to me at Randolph Post Office in Randolph County State of Indianna North America and I shall get it. My dear Temperance and Richard Charleton says they must have their love sent to thee.

Bibliography

John Bright, the life of, by G. M. Trevelyan (Constable & Co. Ltd. 1913/14)

John Bright and the Quakers (2 vols.) by J. Travis Mills (Methuen & Co. Ltd. 1935)

Robert Charleton, memoir by Anna F. Fox (Samuel Harris & Co. 1873)

Journal of the Friends Historical Society Vol. 52, No. 2 (1969) pp 78-96 The Quaker Deputation to Russia by Stephen Frick

London Friends' Institute, Bishopsgate, Biographical Catalogue (West Newman & Co. 1888)

Henry Pease, the father of English Railways, diaries of, by Sir Alfred E. Pease, Bart (Headley Brothers 1907)

Henry Pease, A short story of his life by Mary H. Pease (Headley Brothers 1898)

Mary Pease, A memoir by Marion E. Fox (printed for private circulation, Hatchards 1911)

Pierremont Days by Marion E. Fox (printed for private circulation, Hatchards 1938)

Quaker Biographies, Vol. 5 pp 95-118 includes a short life of Joseph Sturge by Lily Sturge (Friends Book Store, Philadelphia 1914)

Quaker Experiences in International Conciliation by C. H. Mike Yarrow (Yale University Press 1978)

Quakers in Peace and War by Margaret E. Hirst (Swarthmore Press Ltd. 1923)

Quakers in Russia by Richenda C. Scott (Michael Joseph 1964)

The Story of Quakerism 1652-1952 by Elfrida Vipont (The Bannisdale Press)

Memoirs of Joseph Sturge by Henry Richard (Partridge & Bennett 1884)

Joseph Sturge by Stephen Hobhouse (J. M. Dent & Sons Ltd. 1919)

Manuscript Sources	*Periodicals and Papers*
Catherine Charleton's notebook	The Friend
Robert Charleton's letters	The London Illustrated News
Meeting for Sufferings' Minutes	Punch
Henry Pease's Letters	The Times